POLITICS
AND
LITERATURE

POLITICS AND LITERATURE

Jean-Paul Sartre

Translated by J.A. Underwood,
John Calder

CALDER & BOYARS
LONDON

First published in Great Britain
in these translations from the French in 1973
by Calder and Boyars Ltd
18 Brewer Street London W1R 4AS

Myth and Reality in the Theatre first published
in this translation in the magazine *Gambit*

The essays and interview in this book
first appeared in the following magazines:
Le Point:
Théoricien en Bolivie, L'Intellectuel Face à la Revolution,
Mythe et Réalité du Théâtre, Une Structure du Langage
Revue d'Esthétique:
L'Ecrivain et sa langue

ISBN 0 7145 0823 3 Cloth Edition

Typeset in Great Britain by
Specialised Offset Services Ltd, Liverpool
and printed by Biddles Limited, Guildford

Contents

ERRATUM

page 91; Lines 15 to 21 should read:

The way in which you have just described the relationship of signification to the thing signified — in which moreover you referred to a work of Merleau-Ponty's written at a time when he was himself under the influence of Heidegger —

A Theoretician in Bolivia

(From an interview with Jean-Claude Garot)

Certain ascetics of proletarian militancy have taken exception to the 'exorbitant' privileges enjoyed by Régis Debray in the context of a struggle and a defeat in which he should have been on the same footing as any other defeated revolutionary.

Their remarks are a further manifestation of the puritanical moralism motivating certain representatives of the Left. Sick of life in the comfort of the West, they seek to salve their consciences by aping the heroes of populism.

They forget that in time of revolution no party has ever hesitated to draw up hierarchies of the functions and capacities vested in its various members. They forget that in time of revolution theoreticians are in the nature of things scarce, that they cannot anyhow be treated as ordinary militants, and that it is therefore not permissible to forgo any available means in attempting to preserve their lives.

First we learned from the papers that Régis

Debray was dead; then we heard he was alive but had been arrested carrying arms; finally even that pretence was abandoned. We still do not know the charge against him. Yet General Barrientos talks of having him shot – and that in a country where capital punishment has been abolished. He is kept incommunicado: neither his mother, nor the French ambassador, nor his lawyer have been allowed to see him. There is talk of his case being heard *in camera* by a military court. What terrible crime has he committed, then? What can the Bolivian government possibly charge him with? Well, he is the author of a book on revolution. The book was not of course born in a vacuum. It sums up Debray's experiences as acquired in the course of an extended journey through Latin America. In it he declares his solidarity with the Cuban experiment. The main thing he does in it, though, is to trace what he calls the consequences of that lesson for the future. And this, as we shall see, is why he is now under arrest, and possibly under torture as well.

These consequences are as follows. Under certain conditions, i.e. in the Latin-American context, the political process is inseparable from the military process. They form an organic whole. The corresponding organisation is the people's army, the kernel of which is the guerrilla force. The revolutionary party may take the form of the guerrilla cell; the guerrilla cell is the party in gestation. Debray goes on: 'That is why, in order to develop the political *avant-garde*, you must first develop the guerrilla force. That is why the work of insurrection is today's number one political task.'

Which is what bothers the propertied classes of Latin America, and more especially of the United States. The Latin-American countries, where the army is a uniquely repressive force directed against the exploited classes, have always to a greater or lesser extent tolerated the parties of the Left — even if they have from time to time tortured and imprisoned their leaders. The fact is that the Left as a political party is powerless. The urban proletariat is not strong enough to constitute a real force on its own. That was made clear in Bolivia during the 1965 general strike. Regular army units surrounded the mines, the air force bombarded them, and soldiers invaded the workers' homes and gunned down their wives and families. Order was restored. The strike failed because those men, tied to their place of work, were from the word go terribly exposed. Their power had no substance. They had groups organized for self-defence, but these the authorities had no difficulty in wiping out. The guerrilla force, on the other hand — invisible, mobile, disappearing as soon as it has struck, operating out of reach of any air force, simultaneously performing its work of political education among the mass of the peasants, i.e. the most numerous section of the population — that is what Latin-American governments fear most. And another thing: as the history of the last few years has shown, these governments can count on the guerrillas and the parties of the Left falling out amongst themselves from time to time. The latter

are still officially allowed to exist. They have never
been banned. They are more ready to compromise
than the guerrillas. The government in power can
always rely on such differences of opinion dividing
them. Latin-American governments know that
when there is a semblance of left-wing representation in the national assembly or at the local level,
that section of the Left will act as a brake on
partisan activity.

Translated into Spanish, published in Cuba, and
with 200,000 copies printed, Debray's book has
excited considerable interest in Latin America and
has in fact been read and digested by those
elements of the petty bourgeoisie – the students,
for example – from whose ranks the instigators of
the armed struggle in that part of the world are
emerging.

What exactly does the book say? That it is the
guerrilla force itself that must shape its politics,
without reference to – or at any rate not in
subordination to – political parties. The guerrilla
force must create its own politics. There must be
no political commissars in the guerrilla force, only
men who are at one and the same time combatants
and politicians. That is the principal thesis of
Revolution in the Revolution. And it is the man
who put forward this thesis, who has sought to free
the guerrilla force from the brake applied by the
official parties of the Left and to show that the
actual experience of combat teaches that there
must not be two powers but one only – it is this
man who has been arrested, and for precisely that
reason.

But what charges can they possibly bring against him? That he was carrying arms? They have not even bothered to keep up the pretence. That he was active as a political commissar? But his whole book is designed to show that there is no place in the guerrilla force for such foreign elements as political commissars; it is the guerrillas themselves who must weld themselves as a whole, without outside influence, into *political action*, the politics of the armed struggle. That he was attempting to impose policy directives derived from a foreign country — Cuba, for example? Absurd. The book explains precisely that directives as to policy can never be 'imported' from abroad. Debray writes: 'Castroism is simply the concrete process of regeneration of Marxism-Leninism on the basis of Latin-American conditions and the particular historical conditions obtaining in each country. Consequently, it will never present the same appearance twice in any two different countries. In fact it would be a good thing if the word itself were dropped.' Clearly he envisaged a diversification of the armed struggle; in each instance it must be rooted in the conditions obtaining in the country in question.

What was he doing in Bolivia, then? He could be described as a journalist, but theoretician would be nearer the mark. He talks in his book of the necessity for promoting greater effectiveness, adding: 'Effectiveness is not opposed to theory but to the opposition between theory and practice.' His conception of theory and its close relationship to politics, and of the mutual conditioning of the two, meant that as a theoretician he must remain in constant contact with the realities of the Latin-American situation – not in order to become actively involved himself but in order to be able continually to check and to verify his concepts, so that theoretical truths should not, once they are written down, become fixed and immutable, and thus false because overtaken by events. That is his crime. Admittedly, he brought with him his revolutionary opinions, but not to take up arms and participate in the rebellion as a Bolivian revolutionary. He came to study at close quarters the realities of that rebellion. Why arrest him, then? For this reason: a revolutionary, a theoretician of the Latin-American revolution, wherever he may come from and whatever he may do, is, as far as any Latin-American government is concerned, enemy number one. He has got to be stopped before he can provide the revolution in progress all over the continent with a theory or an ideology. That is why Debray has been arrested.

His arrest is intolerable, based as it is on a simple violation of opinion. Certainly Debray called himself, considered himself, and was a Marxist-Leninist. Is that any reason to arrest him and throw him in jail? In our country we still enjoy freedom of opinion. In the name of the freedom we must bring pressure to bear on our government (which has already made certain – extremely half-hearted – approaches to the Bolivian government) to demand that Régis Debray be unconditionally set at liberty.

Revolution and the Intellectual

(An interview with Jean-Claude Garot)

What does the position of 'left-wing intellectual' mean today?

First of all, I don't think you can have an intellectual without his being 'left-wing'. There are of course people who write books and essays and so on and who belong to the Right. As far as I am concerned, though, simply using one's intellect is not enough to make one an intellectual. If it were, there would be no difference between a manual worker and people who read and improve their minds. Where would you draw the distinction between the professional workers of the period of anarcho-syndicalism who sought to think out their situation and an intellectual who wrote essays? The worker works with his hands. But so does the intellectual write with his hands. In this sense there is no distinction. What you have to do in fact is define the intellectual on the basis of the function which society begins by assigning to him. The man I call an 'intellectual' is recruited from a socioprofessional group made up of what one might call the 'theoreticians of practical knowledge'.

This definition stems from the fact that we now know all knowledge to be practical. A hundred years ago it was possible to regard scientific research as being disinterested; that was the bourgeois concept. Today this is an outdated ideology. We know that science sooner or later implies practical application. Consequently, it is impossible to find any kind of knowledge which is, strictly speaking, non-practical. The theoretician of practical knowledge can be an engineer, a doctor, a researcher, a sociologist, etc. The sociologist, for example, studies in the United States how to improve relations between bosses and workers in such a way as to cover up the class struggle. Atomic science, it goes without saying, has an immediate practical application. In other words, as soon as you have a practitioner of some kind who operates on the basis of knowledge (the operational laws of which define his field of activity) for the purpose of obtaining further knowledge, a purpose which is not immediately practical but which may become so, or is so indirectly, as in the case of a doctor — then I would define that man as a theoretician of practical knowledge, but not as an intellectual. What on the other hand defines an intellectual in our society is the deep-seated contradiction between the universality which bourgeois society is obliged to grant his knowledge and the particular ideological and political framework within which he is forced to apply it. A doctor studies blood in so far as 'blood' is a universal reality, i.e. in so far as blood-groups exist everywhere in the same way; hence his theoretical practice constitutes a spontaneous denunciation of racialism. But he is made to study this biological universality in the service of bourgeois society. In this capacity he represents a certain level of the middle-class bourgeoisie which, although not capital-producing, shares a portion of the increment value through helping bourgeois society to survive. The intellectual-to-be has thus received a universal education, but in the context of a particular society with particular interests and possessing a class ideology – an ideology which is itself particular, which is instilled in him from childhood onwards, and the particularity of which is in contradiction to the universalism of his social activity.

The intellectual, however, remains dependent upon his ideology, in so far as it is the ruling class itself which, controlling the purse-strings, decides upon the distribution of jobs and appointments for intellectuals. In other words, the intellectual is a twofold product of bourgeois society: firstly, he is a product of the particular class in power and the particular ideology it holds, which forms him *qua* private individual, and secondly he is a product of the technical universality of a bourgeois society which assigns to the restricted domain of organized science the clear conscience of its *de jure* universalism and thus forms him *qua* universal technician.

You have this curious character, then, a true product of present-day society, who exists in a state of perpetual contradiction between, on the one hand, an ideology instilled in him since childhood and naturally comprising all the characteristic bourgeois concepts — racialism, a certain type of humanism which represents itself as universal but is in fact restrictive — and on the other hand the universality of his profession. If this man compromises, if he turns his back on reality, if by the exercise of bad faith, by performing a kind of balancing act, he succeeds in keeping at bay the uncertainty arising out of this contradiction, then I do not regard him as an 'intellectual'. I regard him simply as a functionary, a practical theoretician of the bourgeois class. Even if he is an author or essayist it makes no difference; he will defend the particular ideology he has been taught.

But as soon as he becomes aware of the contradiction, as soon as his job leads him to challenge, in the name of the universal, the particular within himself and hence everywhere, then he is an intellectual. In other words the intellectual is a man whose peculiar internal contradiction, if he makes that contradiction explicit, causes him to find himself occupying the least favoured positions — that being where universality is generally to be found.

By what theoretical criteria can this intellectual be defined?

The first theoretical criterion they possess comes from their job: it is rationality. For them there is a strict relationship between universality, which is the very product of practical reasoning and dialectics, and the classes which, in a negative sense, uphold the universal. The least privileged classes, as Marx pointed out, can only realize their aims by destroying the very notion of class and creating the social universal. This means that universality is no longer relegated to the apparently irresponsible domain of science but becomes once more the social and historical universality of mankind. Because it is in fact this practical universality which has made possible and inevitable scientific development and the technical accumulation of labour – as an affirmation, which the bourgeois class has appropriated to itself, of man's power over the world.

So the first criterion is that all irrationality be abolished, not from any sentimental point of view, because in fact the only way to abolish the contradiction is to use reason to combat ideology, but from a theoretical point of view which contains within itself the passage to the practical level. In so far as his reason is inherently opposed to racialism, the intellectual is among those who suffer from racialism, and the only way in which he can help them initially is by formulating in and beyond himself a rational critique of racialism.

The second criterion of the intellectual must be radicalism. In the struggle between the particular and irrational and the universal, no compromise is possible; nothing is possible except the *radical* elimination of the particular. The intellectual suggests above all the idea of radical action. And his practical knowledge, because it is practical, can only find its support in social groups which themselves demand radical action.

This means that every time there is a choice to be made in the matter of parties or political groupings the intellectual is impelled to choose whichever is most radical in order to regain universality.

In actual fact we are all, as intellectuals, what one might call universal individuals. That is to say our decisions are still, in spite of everything, tied to a certain number of irrational elements — quite rational, of course, from the point of view of an analysis of our situation in society, but irrational in so far as they are felt and experienced. Consequently there is an element of irrationality that causes options to be arrived at by the mode of the universal individual. But what is certain is that the task of the intellectual lies in freeing himself from his contradiction (which is ultimately the contradiction of society itself) and for that purpose occupying the most radical position. But radicalism can lead us into certain dangers. One of those dangers is 'leftism', i.e. demanding the universal immediately and instantaneously with all the practical, theoretical, and in fact very often symbolic and imaginary consequences which this kind of 'voluntarism' implies. Fortunately in the intellectual's case there are two elements acting as a brake on leftism.

First of all, there is the fact that the intellectual must arrive and wishes to arrive at 'practice' by way of truth. Truth is what action discovers to be the scope of real possibility. The intellectual's action, in so far as he was originally a theoretician of practical knowledge, can only be defined as the

synthetic utilization and determination of possibilities. In the case of an experiment there are
certain possibilities. These are not limited to the
ways in which the equipment can be arranged in
the laboratory; they depend also on the financial
resources which the experimenter has at his
disposal. A doctor has certain possibilities. These
are not only the possibilities of contemporary
medical science; there is also for example the fact
that a particular operation which would best fit the
case cannot be performed because the patient is
not in the right place, i.e. he is way out in the
country, or lying beside a railway line after a train
smash, etc.

In this sense, constant evaluation of the scope of
possibility has the effect of restraining the intellectual and preventing his radicalism from turning
into leftism. Thus an intellectual will never —
unless he has in fact fallen a prey to leftism — say
that the revolution in Belgium or France is coming
tomorrow and that preparations must be made for
an immediate assumption of power.

The politician may say so. A banned French
Communist Party member did in fact say a few
years ago: 'The revolution is at hand; we shall see
socialism in our lifetimes.' He was not speaking as
an intellectual; he was speaking as a 'leftist', for
propaganda purposes. The intellectual's radicalism
will be held in check by his having continually to
take stock of the scope of possibility.

The second check on radicalism, the radical
choice once made, results from a further contradiction. The first contradiction lay between the

irrational and ideological particular on the one
hand and the practical and scientific universal on
the other. The second lies in the opposition
between discipline and criticism. An intellectual, as
soon as he joins a political party, is obliged like
anyone else, or to an even greater extent than
anyone else, to submit to its discipline. At the
same time, however, his peculiar nature, in so far as
he judges the particular in terms of the universal,
compels him to be critical. Intellectuals in socialist
societies face exactly the same problem.

There are thus two checks on the tendency to
leftism: concern for truth and respect for discipline. These two checks stem from a double
contradiction which must be resolved dialectically;
on the one hand, the contradiction which causes
the theoretician of practical knowledge to become
an intellectual (that between particular and universal), and, on the other hand, the contradiction
between the practical aims of the party and the
universal vocation which is what attracted the
intellectual to the party (the antithesis of discipline
and criticism).

It is as if the same particularity as motivated the
intellectual's rational radicalism were reborn within
the party — despite the fact that the latter
represents itself as the instrument most apt to
realize that radicalism. But since in this case the
particularity of the party is put forward purely
with a view to the universal and not in opposition
to it, as in bourgeois society, the intellectual will
agree to place himself under its discipline — while
remaining alert to the risks of rightist deviation and

the danger of losing sight of long-term objectives.

Now then, intellectuals who have gone over to leftism through universality are still intellectuals — but mistaken intellectuals. They elected to go the whole hog. They opted from the start for a group which appeared to them to represent the universal. They examined neither the real possibilities of that group's situation *nor the implications of loyalty*.

But it may be that now a different group represents the universal. This gives rise to very serious problems because before switching parties one must first of all find out, in the context of discipline, whether in fact the first party is wrong and whether it would be appropriate to change over to another group.

What is your position with regard to the Chinese 'pole'?
I personally am neither pro- nor anti-Chinese; I neither support the so-called Maoist forces nor do I support the others. And this for one reason and one alone — nothing that I have so far read on the subject has provided me with any satisfactory universal view. I find strong feelings, I find sometimes extremely intelligent interpretation — for example there is a remarkable article by Pierre Verstraeten, but it is a complete shot in the dark: it does not correspond to anything the Chinese authorities or the Red Guards have said or written. Verstraeten has written a work of philosophical imagination which makes it possible to understand what a cultural revolution must be, but not what in fact it is. And the reason we do not know what it is

is very simple: we just do not have access to sufficient information, apart from Chinese sources extremely badly interpreted. On one occasion a poster was put up in Shanghai saying: 'The opposition forces are severing the ears and noses of the Red Guards.' The Western press immediately came out with: 'Torture in hina.' Whereas in fact the poster was employing a form of words which meant simply that the opposition forces were seeking to humiliate the Red Guards. At most the poster told us that there was a struggle going on in Shanghai, but it contained nothing to suggest that that struggle was either violent or bloody. Similarly, the beginning of an article by Po Mo Jo was translated here as: 'I am prepared to roll in the dirt, my work is worthless from start to finish, I roll myself in the dirt, etc.' Whereas it should have been translated, as the Russians more correctly translated it: 'I realize that, even at my age, one must be prepared to get one's hands dirty.' What he meant was: literature ought to be truly of the people, ought to be born of labour, of the work of men's hands. The result is that I find myself confronted with a lot of emotional and of course contradictory interpretations. Many of my Soviet friends see in the Chinese a real evil, namely the primitive Manicheism of a few years back.

Or I find on the other hand analyses which are quite admirable but which ultimately rest on no foundation at all – notably those of the *Cahiers Marxistes-Léninistes*. I think this is the kind of question where many intellectuals are too quick to take sides. Their being intellectuals ought to inhibit them from making up their minds one way or the other because they are supposed to be on the side of truth, i.e. of the strict determination beforehand of the scope of possibility. But here one of the 'possibles' is missing – namely knowledge, information.

Making up your mind with full knowledge of the facts is fine. Making up your mind in a state of ignorance means a backsliding into the particular. It means abandoning the defining criterion of the intellectual, namely that of an attitude enabling one to bring to bear upon the social world and upon every individual in it – the two dimensions being inseparable – a technique of purification and universalization.

Given the evident lack of radicalization in the revolution in Russia at the moment, is it not incumbent on the intellectual to keep a sharply critical eye trained on that quarter? In other words, are the criteria of revolutionary practice still recognizable in the USSR?

Clearly, in so far as we can know anything of the evolution of the Soviet world, the intellectual must be critical and must look for the foundations on which Soviet practice is based. The very principles of the intellectual being universality and radicalization, the revolution, which is the condition and at the same time the unity of those two objectives, must be permanent – not necessarily in the Trotskyist sense but in the quite prosaic sense that the struggle has begun and is not yet over. No country is entitled, having achieved prosperity, to cease from that struggle; in doing so, it would be defining a universality which was localized and therefore false, because universality must be on the scale of the whole world. One sees that certain constituent elements of the class struggle have shifted position and thus altered its field of application. Struggles become struggles between one country and another rather than within one country between the structures of society and the groups resulting from them.

Seen in this context, it is possible to ask whether Russian society does still constitute a revolutionary whole. Such an analysis must be made rationally, and hence, intellectually speaking, from a Marxist point of view. Because if the intellectual wants to look rationally at society he must first remove his own contradiction, and for this he can only make use of Marxism.

For myself, on the basis of such knowledge as I have of the USSR, I deduce the following: the revolutionary idea became incarnate in 1917 and this necessarily involved its being put into practice in terms of the world, as well as a constant risk of deviation stemming from outside and even from within the undertaking itself. I note that certain contradictions became apparent immediately — for example the absolute necessity for a crash programme of industrialization, which in turn necessitated setting up a major demographic current, bringing untrained peasants into the working class, perpetually reconstituting that class on the basis of fresh elements, lowering the tone of Marxism to turn it into an instrument of propaganda, and at the same time the necessity of creating a clearly differentiated and structured whole which should be the proletariat invested with its dictatorship. The result of this contradiction was that it was impossible for the proletariat to exercise that dictatorship: the manner in which the proletariat was constituted militated against the effective exercise of power.

To make the system work, substitutes had to be found; privileges and rewards had to be created, wage differentials increased, etc. Whereas in principle the aim was quite the opposite, namely to eliminate want and its attendant social inequalities. The effect of this has been to create a broad bureaucratic stratum in Soviet society — but its significance lies not so much in the abstract criticism that may be levelled against the 'essence' of the bureaucracy; it has a bearing on the social set-up as a whole, because this stratum is in its way a reflection of structures, of individuals, of the workers themselves. The danger is of the USSR turning into the curious phenomenon of a petty-bourgeois world based not on private but on state capitalism. And it seems to me that this is obviously something the intellectual ought to be concerned about. On the other hand, the USSR does quite clearly still represent the country that abolished the private ownership of the tools of labour.

So it is not possible to adopt so critical an attitude towards the USSR as would lead one to break off relations with it. It is a question of examining the situation minutely and, in so far as an intellectual can influence a process — and that is not very far — exerting such influence by encouraging every kind of progress and avoiding every danger, that is to say by upholding very firmly a correct representation of principles. The intellectual differs from the politician in that his theoretical action ought to be the revolutionary action's safeguard against every possible deviation.

That is why breaking with the USSR on the pretext of an absolute and unconditioned critical posture or in the name of a pure and immediate demand for universality seems to me to. be a mistaken attitude and one which represents a mistaken resolution of the fertile contradiction between discipline and criticism. Anyone taking such a step would be failing to establish the field of real possibility which constitutes the initiative of the USSR on the basis of its past and what it has already made of its past. Consequently he would be falsifying the truth, i.e. effective analysis of the situation, in the name of a 'critical' desire to defend that universality, and so placing in opposition to one another the two essential qualities of the intellectual, namely truthfulness and radicalism.

On the other hand, loyalty to the USSR as a country which has taken over the means of production, which has perhaps not got beyond the stage of 'pre-socialism' even today, but which at any rate is in possession of the 'concept' of socialism and as such represents the reality of socialism in a more or less adequate fashion since it does in spite of everything possess revolutionary elements — this kind of loyalty, based on this kind of analysis, cannot be wholly negative. Looked at in this way, breaking with the USSR makes no sense at all. What is needed is the kind of dialectical loyalty which I have just described.

For the same reason it is impossible to accept without reserve the Chinese position, in so far as that position is critical of Russian society. Firstly because its criticisms are themselves political and emotional, even if some of them are extremely well-founded, and secondly because the role of the intellectual, unless he is wholly convinced — and such will only be the case after long and agonized debate — does not consist in darting about from camp to camp on the pretext that this one is more radical or that one is doing more for the under-developed countries, and so on. On the contrary, his role is to maintain a position in which he seeks to discover the possibilities of recon-struction of a socialist world, even if, for the time being, reality seems to be against it, and in any case to look upon the given realities in terms of a field of possibility, notably as regards the relationship possible between the Chinese and the Russians. The attitude adopted by some of the Japanese writers I met in Japan is an extremely interesting one, although I do not know how long they are going to be able to keep it up. They visit their Chinese friends with the greatest regularity, and then, a year or six months later, or even travelling straight on from China, they go and see their Soviet friends. They reason as follows: 'It is not for us to denounce either one or the other because

that sets up particularities. Our job is to try and
discover a universal on the basis of which both
points of view will be, if not reconcilable, at least
comprehensible.' This is what Gorz does so well in
Le socialisme difficile. He shows that the special
position of European communists implies at the
moment that to a certain extent they adopt the
policy of the USSR, i.e. that of the developed
countries, but that on the other hand, with regard
to revolutionary strategy as a whole, it is clear that
the elements of revolution are more developed,
notably as regards the Third World, in the Chinese
position.

*Does Cuba constitute a primary revolutionary pole
comparable with the Chinese and Russian poles?*
It is absolutely impossible for an intellectual not to
be pro-Cuban. This chaotic revolution has had its
negative moments but it does possess a direction
which it has followed, a direction which is and
continues to be a radical one. It is equally
impossible not to adopt a position of solidarity
with regard to the relationships which Cuba is
embarking upon in Latin America. On the other
hand, it is impossible to apply the Cuban revolutionary stance to our historical situation as a
whole. The kind of action undertaken in Cuba,
wholly justifiable in the South American context,
cannot without modification be imported here.
Thus one can extend one's complete solidarity to a
complex of revolutionary countries and feel that
they have accomplished the most radical action
without this obliging one to reproduce the same

kind of radicalization here. The reason being that they started out from a partial misreading of the problem which justified their radicalization but at the same time made it impossible to transpose that radicalization word for word elsewhere.

For them the primary objective was the army. This was already a radical position as compared with many states of Latin America. In fact the majority of left-wing groups in those states believe that the army can be won over to the Left by packing it with loyal popular elements. The first radical breakthrough was the realization that as long as the army's power of coercion remained unbroken, healthy government would be impossible. 'Even for us,' Fidel once told me. 'If we had assumed power on the basis of a compromise we would have been corrupted, for all our good intentions.'

This attitude with regard to the army was the first radicalization. The second lay in the discovery of American interests behind the army. Fidel started by opposing Batista, and by the very radicalism of his action he quickly came to see that behind Batista stood the power of the army, and behind the power of the army stood the power of America. The logic of radicalism is implacable. It is this kind of radicalization that the Americans are up against today in Vietnam.

A perfect situation, then, but one which for us Europeans should serve not as an example, not as a model, not as a figurative and literal lesson, but as a dialectical type of rationalization and radicalization. It has been claimed that Guevera told

Debray: 'Go home to France and create guerrilla armies there.' The claim is absurd. Guevara can have said no such thing because Guevara knew very well that the situation of the industralized nations does not call for the guerrilla army as a precondition of revolution. Moreover Debray explains this quite clearly in his book: 'Castroism is each movement in Latin America discovering the truth of Marxism, through warfare, and in its own territory.' Castroism has nothing to offer but an example of radicalization.

Is this kind of critical analysis not excessively theoretical and does it not practically speaking condemn the Western intellectual to inaction? What can the revolutionary intellectual do in Western countries, France in particular?

The first and essential task here in France is precisely that of critical analysis. There are various ways of looking at this. It is a useful exercise to write books and articles denouncing without passion but with rigorous objectivity the whole mumbo-jumbo of the technocratic class and the consumer society which it preaches, and combating the pseudo-scientific literature published on this subject – combating it, exposing it, and if need be making use of the mass media to put across explanations which are easy to understand but which must not stoop to the level of mere vulgarization.

The second approach would consist of an analysis of France's actual situation – its economic dependence on the USA, its so-called policy of independence whereas the only possible policy of independence would be an economic policy which sought to develop French capital (within a class struggle, of course) in opposition to the American capital at present dominating our economy. The intellectual would firstly combat false *interpretation* of the economic situation, that is to say he would combat the ideology of bourgeois society by exposing the particularity behind its pretence of universality, by exposing its role, its theology of class, and secondly he would try to show the *actual situation*, i.e. the precise situation in which France finds herself today. This is a point of view which I regard as being specifically intellectual in so far as it is a critical one. I do not think it is the intellectual's job to make suggestions on the level of exact programmatic objectives — that is the job of the Party — but what the intellectual can do in addition is try to re-define a certain number of principles which have got blown to pieces today, namely the principles of the revolution.

Do any revolutionary models exist outside revolution? Similarly, can there be any theoretical demythologization outside action?
Theoretical demythologization and action are one and the same. Demythologization is something that can only be done on behalf of a group of people who are at the same time engaged in some kind of practical action. This is why I said that one of the difficulties facing the intellectual, one of his contradictions, is that he is not much liked by parties in so far as parties are political formations

and as such tend sometimes to opt for possibilities which make them deviate from a radical line. The intellectual must assert principles. Moreover, he can only develop his practical knowledge by placing himself at the service of people who desire universality as he does. Subsequently his task within the group is to be continually reminding the group of its goals, the ultimate goal being a universalist society, and if need be he must point out that a particular deviation may seriously compromise the future.

But what precise course of action is the intellectual to put forward?
I was coming to that. In the first place the intellectual, in association with the whole of the group he represents, has to try and re-think the notion of revolution — as Gorz is doing, as the Italian Communist intellectuals are doing — particularly with a view to finding out whether we really are faced with the single dilemma of revolution/reformism — accepting that reformism means abandoning revolution in favour of a policy of class collaboration, and that on the other hand revolution as defined fifty or sixty years ago in the wake of events cannot occur again in the same way and does not constitute an imminent likelihood in the West. In this context books like Gorz's are indispensable. There is mythologization in the world of revolution too; when a person calls himself a revolutionary, it does not necessarily make him one. The problem today is one of knowing exactly what revolution represents. We

know the goal — to create a classless society in place of present-day society by setting up a provisional dictatorship of the working class on the basis of elements — destroyed to a greater or lesser extent but still in existence — of the previously dominant classes. So the problem is not one of knowing how to achieve revolution in the present situation but one of knowing how to set about approaching it. Now, what does this mean in the long run for the groups of parties or trade-unions which constitute the working classes as a whole, and in what can the theoretical-practical revolutionary stance consist? In France it means bringing about the union of the Left on the basis of a common programme. This is an essential task. It is a mistake to think that radicalism consists in rejecting all the forces of the Left on the grounds that they happen to be terribly divided and very often represent mutually irreconcilable interests. On the contrary, it is a question of creating the only possibility for struggle.

But the intellectual is no politician. He must push the party towards the programme of which he has laid down the broad outlines, but it is not his job to get down to working out the precise, concrete details. The intellectual must continually uphold a certain number of radical principles, together with all the extensions of those that he is able to draw. At the time of the Algerian war he would say that this is a colonialist war and he would say how far it ought to be opposed and by what practical means — inciting the troops to desert, and so on. But when it comes to defining

the terms on which the FLN shall negotiate with
de Gaulle, that is none of his business. His task is
to say one·thing and one only — that the French
should get out. How they should do so and what
should be the nature of the subsequent relations
between the two countries are other matters
entirely — on condition that the principle of
relations of independence be upheld.

*You have invoked a minimal platform. Can our
capitalist society be sufficiently changed through
the agency of the traditional unions of left-wing
parties to make it possible to opt for this solution
rather than the revolutionary struggle? This idea of
progressive change, of peaceful co-existence, may
lead us to capitulate before permanent and
escalating aggression on the part of the Americans.
Do we have to make a choice between changing
capitalist society and radical action? For example,
if the Americans decided to invade Cuba
tomorrow, what attitude ought the Left to adopt?
Where is the line that must not be over-stepped in
this hope of changing and reforming capitalist
society?*

In my opinion that line has already been overstep-
ped on many occasions. The job of the Left — and
this is what the Left does not realize — is to create
a revolutionary situation first of all by more or less
legal means, i.e. by strikes, by voting. If the Left
seizes power, then — at that moment — it finds
itself in a revolutionary situation, not *vis-a-vis* its
own bourgeoisie but *vis-a-vis* American imperial-
ism.

At the moment, however, in France, the ideas put forward by left-wing politicians are very much toned down. They are afraid of rubbing the bourgeoisie up the wrong way and only propose to nationalize a few industries by way of concessions to the Communist Party. So they are not going to go very far in terms of action. They will try and govern, and they will step down if they are 'democratically' defeated at the next election. What kind of prospect does this offer?

No, what I think will happen is this: as soon as they start anything they will become involved in a conflict, latent at first but which will soon become international. The reason is that revolutionary situations tend nowadays to be created more by the Right than by the Left; counter-revolution flares up where one only expected to see a movement of peaceful reform. I am thinking of the example of Greece. I don't mean to say that the Greeks were particularly revolutionary. They wanted a democracy that worked. The boldest among them wanted the king to abdicate so as to have a proper bourgeois democracy, but many of them would have been happy with a centre government with the king abstaining from the exercise of power or giving his blessing. You saw how even that position was untenable, since the USA immediately organized a *coup*. Greece is not all that far away from us; we cannot say to ourselves: 'It will never happen here.' That is what people said about Poland in 1939, and what they say now about Vietnam. But Greece has brought it home to us: it could happen here.

Le Point, no. 13, January 1968

Myth and Reality in the Theatre

It is no longer possible to talk of the theatre today, considering the success of Ionesco, Beckett, Adamov, Jean Genet, Peter Weiss and especially Bertolt Brecht, as we would have done before these playwrights came on the scene. The basic question before us is whether or not the theatre has undergone a real revolution since the appearance of what we call 'the new theatre'.

In fact, no, there has not been a revolution, because these new authors, who appear from different horizons and who have different preoccupations cannot be classified with a single epithet. In particular they have been called creators of a 'theatre of the absurd'. This appellation is itself absurd because not one of them considers human life or the world as an absurdity. Certainly not Genet, who studies the interrelationship between reality and fantasy; nor Adamov, who is a Marxist and has written, 'No theatre without ideology'; nor even Beckett, of whom we will talk a little later. What they actually represent, whether it is in their interior conflicts or in their reciprocal contradictions, is the explosion of those contradictions that lie at the very heart of the theatrical art. Indeed there is no art which does not possess a morass of contradictions in its contemplation of its 'unity' and 'quality'. The modern novel is full of contradictions and of presuppositions which destroy each other. And the theatre has contradictions of its own, which have up to now passed in silence.

For years and even centuries, the theatre has played the double role of being the theatre and of also being the cinema for those who had need of the cinema, but who did not yet know what this could be, as it had not yet been invented. In making its appearance, the cinema, contrary to popular belief, has *not* created a crisis for the theatre, nor has it negated the theatrical art. It has negated the work of some theatrical producers in reaching the public; it has negated a certain kind of theatre, that kind which occupies the role of the cinema, that is to say the bourgeois realistic theatre, whose purpose is to give an exact reproduction of reality; and it negated it from the moment when realism in films became superior to theatrical realism. A tree for a cinema-goer is a real tree, while a tree on the stage is obviously synthetic. And so the cinema has denounced the synthetic theatrical tree as a simple decoration, and the theatrical action as a simple gesture. But the theatre has not been negated, and, on the contrary, from that moment the theatre began to reconsider its proper limitations, and, as in all art, it found its new possibilities from a realisation of its restrictions.

After what Nietzsche called the *Death of God*, and after the death of *inspiration* in the sense of 'God talking in your ear', we have become familiar since Flaubert with the *critical novel* and since Mallarmé with a *critical poetry* which is to say with an art containing the artist's introspective relationship with himself. The coming of the cinema and of various social changes since 1950 has created what we can call *The Critical Theatre*.

These authors whom I am going to study in their various points of difference and resemblance to each other, I consider to be all representatives of the *Critical Theatre*. All of them want to make instruments of communication out of the theatre's own limitations, for example, out of unreality: the gesture on stage appears to many to be a specifically theatrical convention. It is fortunately the gesture and not the action it represents that is seen in the theatre. By the same token, the work of these writers, which is a reflection on the theatre itself, is translated into their work, where it creates a tension between the work of each of them and each of them and his work, because each of them specifically chooses one of the contradictory aspects of the theatre. This is true to the extent that in examining these writers we shall be able to see what kinds of contradictions exist in the dramatic art itself and how each one can be defined in relationship to the others: we are therefore going to examine the nature of those internal forces that oppose each other in modern dramatic representation.

The Gesture or the Action?

The first opposition that we observe is the opposition that exists between the *ceremony* and the unique determinism of a performance. Having progressed in Europe from popular demonstrations, and in the East from ritual songs and dances, the theatre, once formalised, must retain its ceremonial character, as Jean Genet would wish it today, and as the classical French writers made it by writing in verse. Within this perspective we have to communicate with the public through the hypnotic appeal that certain rites produce. Jean Genet's play *The Blacks* is quite simply a black mass. The effect it has on a white member of the public is one of unease, which is the author's intention. Slow incantations prepare us for an act of sacrifice, which is in fact never carried out as it is the imaginary murder of a young white woman. Which is to say that nothing happens. One of the characters says: 'We have the politeness, learned from you, to make communication impossible. The distance which originally separated us will be augmented by our omissions, our manners, and our insolence, because we are also actors.' So briefly, the black who is reproached by whites, unable to communicate because of the white's refusal to communicate, still wishes to play out the comedy to the end. He is himself in real life a theatrical subject. He acts a play and he acts it because the play, as Genet would have it, is imposed by the whites, but has become second nature. In fact the choice of subject has become both introspective and critical. Genet has not looked for a good subject or a good plot, but wished to re-establish the theatre with all its power and its limitations by choosing characters who, in his own terms, can only make a statement in life through the theatre. And as their dramatic actions, the actions of blacks, are a repetition and exaggeration of the roles in which others, namely the whites, have cast them, they will not change, the dramatic elements and the ceremonial elements becoming one and the same. A ceremony is created by repetition. And so, what we want to suggest to the public by this unaltering ritual, this act of sacrifice which is in fact not taking place, is the disappearing presence of the black who hides his black truth at the same time as he manifests it. Because an actor who plays the comedy on the stage, by virtue of the fact that we also make him play it in real life, shows us, in some part, his truth in that way, but by the same token he partly hides it. We do not know what this actor is in the depths of his own being, and it is just the discomfort of knowing this, of realizing that the actor if more than an actor, that creates our sense of anxiety and makes us ill at ease. The longer a black plays the part that we want him to play, the more we think in depth about him: his revolt exists, his armed insurrection exists and his self-affirmation as a man exists through the killings of his settler-executioners.

And so, through the identification of theatre and ceremony in the persons of black actors (who

are really actors because that is their profession —
they are a company of black actors; but who are at
the same time falsely actors, because that is the
requirement of the persons they play; who are
fictitiously in revolt, as the black represent a
hidden revolt; and who are really in revolt because
the blacks manifest their African identity as
opposed to the settlers), Jean Genet elaborates his
work with the purpose of negating his audience.
The ceremony possesses the spectators and gradually leads them to negate themselves.

It is characteristic of the contradiction that I am
at present considering, but now from the other
side, that Antonin Artaud, author of *The Theatre
and its Double*, has never had so many disciples as
at present, and many young writers in France and
abroad consider him to be the principal prophet of
the modern theatre. For Artaud, ceremony is not
emphasised for its characteristic quality of repetition; on the contrary, he instantly sees in a
dramatic performance another quality, its fragility
(a performance is a happening: an actor's loss of
memory can bring stage action to an abrupt halt)
and its unique character. Every evening a performance is improvised with the actors playing well or
badly according to their preoccupations and
according to the disposition of the public, because
there are days according to Jean Cocteau 'when the
public has genius' and others when the public is
bad. And so, depending on whether an actor plays
well or badly, or even one day well and one day
badly, and depending on how much interest the
public shows in a plot, a character or some aspect

of the play in hand, the dramatic balance and the meaning of the play changes from day to day. According to Artaud, from this point of view it is the cinema and not the theatre which is repetitious. Every evening in the cinema, the projectionist shows the same reels, the actors play with the same amount of talent or without talent, and the only accidents which can interrupt the projection are technical ones, not dependent on contact between the actors and the public. In 1928 Artaud's sense of the uniqueness and fragility of a theatrical performance led him to write: 'The theatre seeks to become verily an act open to all solicitations and to all change of circumstances, where chance will always reclaim its rights. A production or a play will always be subject to caution and to revision to such an extent that if the public come several times on different nights they will never see the same performance.' It is therefore a question of thinking of a theatrical performance as something that can never be recaptured. The ceremony that consists of repetition gives place to the unique adventure of every day. It is the equivalent of a 'jam session' in music as compared to a jazz record.

The principle difference between Genet and Artaud, in spite of them both sharing certain Brechtian characteristics, is immediately apparent. Artaud has in fact written in the same text: 'A theatrical production will come to be as passionately involving as a card game in which all the spectators take part.' Genet on the other hand wants to cast a spell over the spectators while keeping them at a distance. In this sense the distance that Brecht and Genet wish to maintain between the spectator and the actor does not exist for Artaud. The underlying reason is that Artaud assigns to the theatre the function of liberating by means of a 'magical operation', as he puts it, the secret powers that are within each member of the public: his libido, his sexual obsessions, his concern with death and violence, all of which must be suddenly released from the whole audience. This is why Artaud came to call his theatre *the theatre of cruelty*, although he never achieved a realisation of it.

This contradiction between Genet and Artaud corresponds accurately to the two contradictory aspects of the theatre, as they represent, at the same time, ceremonial repetition, and vivid drama that is different on each occasion; the world of the theatre keeps us at a distance much more than the world of the cinema, but at the same time we participate through identification with such and such a character. But the opposition between the two goes much further, and it is possible, in looking deeper, to uncover a new contradiction.

Artaud says to us: 'I consider the theatre to be an act.' And, in fact, if we place ourselves in the shoes of the author and the producer, the theatre, that is to say dramatic representation, is an act and a real one. Writing a play is work, so is mounting it, and the purpose of this work is to impose a real action on the public. On its lowest level, and taking for example the theatre of consumption, this action consists of bringing in as many people as

possible and producing in economic terms a profit
for the theatre. And on its highest level, we hope
to bring about, for at least the duration of the
play, if it is designed to produce a sense of scandal,
a certain transformation in the mind of the
spectator. But it is also true that if we put
ourselves in the place of the audience, the play is a
piece of imagination. In other words, without even
excepting historical plays from the argument, the
spectator never loses his realisation that what he is
seeing is unreal. This woman does not really exist,
that man who is her husband is only apparently so;
he does not really kill her. This means that the
spectator does not believe, in the real sense of the
word, in the killing of Polonius. If he did he would
run away or leap upon the stage. Nevertheless he
does believe, or he would not be moved, cry and
wriggle in his seat. But his belief is itself imaginary.
So it is not profound and vital conviction, but an
auto-suggestion which also contains the complete
realization that it is an auto-suggestion.

The result is that the sentiments ensuing from
this participation in the imaginary, from the
presentation of the imaginary on the stage, are
themselves imaginary sentiments. They are felt at
the time as being definite but not real, which
makes it possible for the spectators to feel
frightened when going to see a play which deals in
horror, and at the same time they are not
necessarily indicative of the spectator's real feelings. We know that *Uncle Tom's Cabin* when
played on the stage during the last century made
slave-owners cry while viewing the play, but these

same men in no way changed their behaviour or moral view of their rights regarding negroes after the end of the performance.

Justice becomes Evil

This new contradiction between the act and the gesture, between the real happening and the imaginary persuasion creates different outlooks for those whom we think of as modern dramatists. Genet does not see any disadvantage in his play being considered imaginary, but sees it as a positive quality. The words that he has written about *The Balcony* are equally true of all his other plays. He writes 'Do not perform this play as if it were a satire of this or that. It is the glorification of the imaginary and of the reflection of reality. It's meaning, whether satirical or not, will appear only in this context.' This radical position is identical to Genet's fundamental research into the nature of man himself. For him, a writer who is evil and a thief, who has been condemned by society from the beginning, the unreal and evil itself are the same thing. He is the enemy of those honest people who have condemned him from childhood to existing as an imaginary person and he avenges himself in his plays by confronting these same people with illusions that trap them in an inferno of imaginary reflections that he has woven for them. Briefly, his real purpose as an author is to force good to become for a few hours an imaginary evil, which makes it a double trap. First of all because he forces the practical man, sitting in the theatre, to become unreal himself and to penetrate

the imaginary as if he himself had fallen into evil.
And secondly he puts good people in the position
of imagining their opposites, by identifying themselves with them, so that at the end of the play he
reproaches himself for his own acceptance of evil.
Because the point is this, for Genet the imaginary
is the public's acceptance of real evil, with good
and evil juxtaposed, the spectator still left with his
good conscience, but now carrying away with him
a profound anxiety as well, which he cannot lose.

Brecht is also satisfied with the imaginary, but
for very different reasons. He wants to show, that
is to say take to pieces and seize, the inner dialectic
of a process. All the public's real feelings, of horror
or of fear, for example, contribute to this
information. The spectator must be sufficiently
involved in the action for him to see beyond the
stage action itself. *The Good Woman of Setzuan* is
not a demonstration, but a delightful fable which
does not make the audience afraid, or feel any
other violent sentiment, either of sexual stimu-
lation or of direct emotion or anything else, and
which therefore allows them, at the same time as
they are entertained, to understand the impossibility of doing good in a society which is founded
on exploitation. And so, the imaginary is for
Brecht a bridge between reason and his objective.
That is why he is not afraid to denounce the
imaginary endlessly on the stage as the unreality it
is. He gives us visual conventions, such as corpses
that are in fact dummies and that we see to be
dummies, intentionally so that we are not filled
with horror by the resemblance between a corpse

and a living actor lying on the ground; some of the characters wear masks and others do not; songs are sung between the scenes to signify the subjective nature of the character; constantly he denies us emotion, any break-down, any ultimate in stage excitement. The difference here between Genet and Brecht is that Genet makes the imaginary an end in itself. The sense of theatre lies in the fact that the essential value of the theatre is to represent something that does not exist. Brecht only does this on a minimal basis. But in any case we want to have the unreal sentiment for both cases. On the one hand we want the unreal sentiment in order to believe in it as with Genet, and on the other hand as with Brecht, we make the sentiments unreal so that our passions do not influence our rational conviction. On the other hand, and this is the other side of the contradiction, Artaud, as we have seen (and he was a fellow-traveller with the realists) is not happy with these results, which he considers inadequate. He wants the representation on stage to become an action. He understands the action in the full meaning of the word, and he does not want this activity to consist of producing something which is unreal. The purpose of the theatre is to create in the awareness of each spectator a profound sense of reality. Starting from this intention, a play disintegrates insofar as it is conventional or classical, and the more it contains of plot and of décor, the more this is true, because the surreal sense that we want to produce is based on the principle that there is no difference between the real and the imaginary, a debatable principle, but which has the effect of reducing the fictional element to a minimum and of bringing all the real factors to play in a realistic fashion upon the spectator. For instance, in *The Theatre and its Double*: 'Among the musical instruments should be included a whole variety of objects, because the necessity of playing directly and effectively on the organs of sound reception leads us to seek qualities and vibrations of sound to which we are completely unaccustomed. We must also seek new methods of lighting so that lighting becomes an essential part of the action and new vibrations are set up.' I could cite twenty other such quotations, which indicate the necessary research which is essential to excite the spectator by inducing a sense of reality. We might ask why it is necessary to conserve any semblance of fiction at all under these conditions. Artaud in one of his plays wanted to take the conquest of Mexico as a theme. Why should this pre-conceived theme be worth his while, however great the variations from one day to another in his unreal abstraction, when real sounds and real lights could condition us in a superior manner? If the theatre, as Artaud says, is not an art, if it liberates as a real action does, terrible forces sleeping within us, the spectator is in fact an actor who believes in his acting, who without hesitation would himself join the dance with all the violence that the dance will release in him, then Artaud is stopped at the outset. Because to be logical we must put the spectator along with Artaud quite simply in the presence of a real event, so that his belief is total, and in this sense the theatre of cruelty in a contemporary setting leads to what we call the *Happening*.

The Happening or Documentary Theatre

With the *Happening*, and they have now been performed in France, Britain, America, even in Japan, what is happening is that a real event is taking place. No stage is necessary and a happening can take place in a room or the middle of a hall, in the street or beside the sea, between spectators and those whom we no longer think of as actors but as agents. There is a provisional difference of time. These agents have to actually do something, it matters little what, but something provocative, which causes a real event to happen which can be anything at all. There are some performances that play on waiting, or boredom, in order to liberate something in the spectator. A classic example is for a man to come in, he being the agent. We watch him, not knowing what he is going to do, then he sits on a chair and stays there with arms crossed for two hours, . . . and what happens is that boredom provokes the audience to violent reactions which go as far as tears. It is even possible to directly provoke the sexual instincts. In Paris, for example, a happening was banned because on the stage there was a naked woman covered entirely with whipped cream where the audience could lick up the cream. At other times the fear of death and of violence has been evoked. I saw a happening where cocks had their throats cut and the blood was thrown at the audience. The interest of this affair was not

very great as what was going to happen was largely
foreseen, because before cutting the cocks' throats
you have to first buy them, but the reaction of the
public was nevertheless very real. At the beginning
there is nearly always a scandal, then the audience
divides between those who are in favour and those
who are against such series of violent events; then,
in some cases, you evoke profounder feelings, of
sexuality, or of loss of sexual inhibition, of the
desire for death and so on. And then some kind of
unity takes hold of both spectators and the actors.
For example, one happening in Paris ended as a
protest against the war in Vietnam without anyone
knowing why, because no-one had come to make a
protest.

In this way a *happening* is real. It exists and it
gives an effective opportunity to certain kinds of
mass reactions, which we can take as fact. The
problem really is: what happens to the performance insofar as it is an appeal to the free
imagination of the spectator? Is not this spontaneous bringing of something into being by means
that are more or less cruel the very opposite of
theatre, or rather is it not the moment when the
theatre destroys itself? Most of the time happenings are a carefully thought out exploitation of the
cruelty that Artaud advocates. In France Lebel in
his happenings exposes the public to a certain
sadism: this is accomplished by bright lights that
come and go, by sounds that are insupportable to
the ear and by the audiences' general contact with
various objects which are usually disgusting. You
have to go to these happenings in old clothes. And

the public for happenings have *reacted* to their own torture.

Can we say that we have gone past the limits of the idea and the essence of the theatre? Peter Brook in England has tried to find a mixture, that is to say a compromise that would contain happenings inside the limits of a play. This he has recently done in *US*, of which the title itself is a provocation because it means at the same time *US* the English and U.S. the Americans, and in the subject matter itself, if there is such a thing, and certainly in the main theme, it is also a direct provocation, because it is of course about the war in Vietnam. By itself this play has no meaning and we cannot call it a play. The performance must take place on a stage before the public and there is a succession of scenes, words, and violent acts without any purpose other than the affective which in the middle of the confusion inspires the two themes of the play.

The first part brings home the horror of the war in Vietnam, while the second part is principally about the impotence of the Left.

What we see is neither real, because after all we are looking at actors acting, nor unreal, as everything that happens makes us aware of the reality of the war in Vietnam. And in spite of everything it is the reality that affects the spectator, because it is the noises, the colours, the movements which finally bring about a certain kind of trance or bewilderment, depending upon the individual. The public are not asked to take part in the performance: they are for the most part kept at a distance. They receive this mixture of broken sketches, interrupted at the moments where an illusion is about to be created, as a blow in the face. And at the end they find themselves before a real event, a real happening, even though this happening is renewed every evening.

For on the stage one of the actors opens a box of butterflies. They are taken out and a hand holding a lighter burns them in its flame. They are burnt alive. This is evidently an allusion to the monks who set fire to themselves and burn themselves alive in Saigon. This happening *is* a happening because something really happens: something alive dies and dies suffering. Nevertheless it is not altogether a happening because the curtain comes down and the spectator, sent back to his solitude, leaves with a confused despair made up of shock, fury and impotence. There has been no conclusion and after all what is there to conclude? It is true that the war in Vietnam is a crime. It is also true that the Left is quite incapable of doing anything. Has it anything to do with the theatre? I think it is really on the borderline where form is only an intermediary and where we can either say 'this is theatre' or 'this is not'. In any case we can say that if it *is* theatre, this situation is an excellent example of what we can call the crisis of the imaginary in the theatre.

And indeed in the same perspective, we can see everywhere this strange contradictory wanting to give the public a fiction which is reality. Those who go to these performances know very well what is happening. The experiments in presenting a 'theatre of fact', in plays like *In the Matter of J. Robert Oppenheimer* which was first performed in Germany and which Vilar has presented in France, are witnesses to an event. In this case, it is not a matter of presenting something that has happened, transposed and re-reconstituted according to the ideas of the author, as in historical plays. It consists of repeating the events themselves and the words that each person really spoke at a given moment.

The result has been the opposite of what is produced by a happening. In the happenings it is finally the real that swallows the imaginary. In the theatre of fact, reality becomes changed into the imaginary: the imaginary absorbs the real. The proof is that this play *In the Matter of J. Robert Oppenheimer* as presented in Germany and as played by Vilar in France became two completely different plays.

Why were they different? Because they reflected in spite of everything the feelings of their authors. The trial at Oppenheimer went on for day after day: for the theatre it was necessary to make a selection from the transcript. This selection is in fact a work of authorship. It is a choice and an option which helps to define the character of Oppenheimer. And so that which was seen in Germany and that which was seen in France have nothing to do with the reconstruction of the Oppenheimer trial. They are both something else, and Oppenheimer himself becomes fictitious because we in France never lost sight of Vilar, a great actor whom we know well who plays the role of Oppenheimer. All of a sudden Oppenheimer is no longer a real person, but becomes fictitious and becomes the role of Vilar. He was not conceived as a real being because after all Vilar was talking French and the trial took place in English. All this we know. All these conventions that we accept readily enough where the naturalistic theatre is concerned, where we see the English talking among themselves and talking in French, is completely acceptable because it *is* theatre. But from the moment when what we are trying to do is present the Oppenheimer trial, all these people who are talking French in order to present a real situation, an American situation, make the whole thing completely unreal. It no longer has anything to do with English or the Americans. And so we have a sort of temporary illusion, and in looking at what is going on, we say 'this is a reduction of the trial; this is a trial which gives the illusion of lasting two weeks, but which in fact only lasts two hours on stage.' In fact the trial in the play is really a symbolic allusion to the trial: a summing up of the trial with its transposition to the stage unveiling its abstract truth and not its realistic reconstitution.

And so, between the theatrical illusion which is absorbed or swallowed by some real and sadistic action imposed on the spectator, as in a happening, and the real event which we recreate in the 'theatre of fact,' which is swallowed by the illusion we create, we find the crisis of the image (theatrical credibility).

In fact, underneath the happening there is always an appeal to the image. This is because at bottom, the event, whatever it is, is symbolic of something else and the real serves to create unreality. I do not have enough space to go into it in detail, but in any case this crisis, even if it has the effect of destroying some theatrical conventions, signifies some progress in thought.

We no longer work on the vague and confused principle of the authors and producers of the past, nor of the philosophy of the old theatre, which led us to think that theatricality essentially implies no differentiation in its big moments between the real and the imaginary. We used to be able to believe that an illusion which was presented and which was accepted as an illusion, would necessarily bring out real feelings among the audience. This is the Greek idea of catharsis. The easy conscience with which Gemier at the beginning of the century made his actors come into the auditorium, and cross it in order to get up on the stage, demonstrates the innocence which authors used to have. They thought at the time that the stage was an illusory place, a mirage, and that the characters who went to it by walking through the aisles, because they shocked the audience, would persuade them of the reality of the play. All of a sudden, for all the men of the theatre of our generation, as we shall soon see, the theatre ceased to be realistic. Because, *we want reality* and to achieve it we have to go to the limit, there being no other way of doing so (we provoke real sentiments by real events), or else we must realise that a dramatic representation has a perfectly illusory character, but in that case as its structure is unreal, it is for this very quality that we have to exploit it, as *the negation of reality* (we shall return to the exact meaning of these words) and not as an imitation of it.

The Theatre of Verbal Meaning or the Theatre of the Unconscious

The final and most obvious contradiction and the most fundamental one concerns the role of language in the theatre. A person in a play is a man or perhaps, as in *Chanticler*, an animal conceived in an anthropomorphic manner. He has all the human characteristics, whether there is a plot or not, and he has to talk because a man talks. Language is therefore one means of dramatic expression. In the classical theatre it is the principal means and a great tragic actor moves very little in our tragedies. He can even stay perfectly still for the length of whole tirades. The verbal incantation by itself, its inflection, its rhythm and the speed with which it is deployed, the manner in which the verse is cut up, the values that are given to each word, all take account of the events that are being lived and the passions and the decisions that are being made. Indeed in the classics the world is seen psychologically: Racine explains through language the world of the mind. With the romantic tradition and the dramatists who were inspired by it, everything became changed. These authors tried to make the whole world a part of language, which is to say that nature itself, that world which surrounds us and which the Germans call the 'Umwelt,' the horizons, the obscure forces which work within us and outside us, must find themselves directly or indirectly presented in the dialogue as conscious meaning, as a reference or as an unconscious super-determination of the message of the play, as for instance silence itself, in this conception, which establishes the sovereignity of language. In France between the two wars we had a kind of theatre which called itself the theatre of silence, whose principal author was J. J. Bernard. But in fact it was a very talkative kind of theatre because in the theatre of silence, language annexed the silence. On the one hand, in practice, in these plays language explained the futile and everyday aspects of life. For example the married couple in *Feu qui reprend mal*, a soldier who returns from the war and his wife who never finds him again completely, enter into empty conversations that are full of unease. But these conversations are expressly intended to refer to a sub-conversation. This is because behind the empty words, in the moments of silence, something is said inaudibly: 'I know that you do not love me anymore, but that is not true. I need a little time, because perhaps I really do love you less, but then the same is true for you,' etc. All this conversation is entirely present in spite of not being said, just as a verbal emphasising of phrases that we hear act as a key to give their real meaning.

And so the theatre of silence is a sort of universal verbalism, a total conquest of the theatrical world by the word. Silence is no longer the danger: we stop speaking because we have nothing further to say or because we have to cough or because we are waiting for the other person to say something. The silence consists of verbally miming a verbal content. To cease speaking is to come to the end of a conversation at the moment when the conflict has been clearly resolved. And so briefly, we can say that about 1950 the theatre had attained its maximum verbal possibilities, by which I mean that everything was in the language. In one sense there was no need of any décor and in fact many authors and producers did without scenery, because the scenery was only an illustration of what was being said. The language of Shakespeare, for example, tells us everything we need to know about the exterior world. That is why it is completely unnecessary to see the sun or to produce flashes when lightning or thunder is indicated. If it has been said, it has been represented. The visual element becomes unnecessary because of the power of the verbal element. Of course there are silent gestures in the theatre: there are certain stage directions, and when you have to kill in the theatre, you have to go through the motions of killing, but all these things (gestures, movements, sometimes sounds) were, as far as the theatre of words is concerned, only an accompaniment: in itself, the theatre is supposed to have said everything. It is for this reason that modern productions have been the most inclined to do away with scenery. Barrault replaces solid objects by pantomime, and he brings objects into being and makes them disappear as soon as the pantomime disappears. In his estimation this is quite enough. In one adaptation of a novel for the theatre he was required in one scene to return home, pass before the doorway of his concierge and climb to the third floor to get to his room. It is quite evident that once in his room, the concierge's flat and the stairs become completely useless to the play and therefore in the way and a nuisance. But a pantomime of words to an invisible concierge and a mimed ascent of the staircase suffice well enough. The solid world is banished through mime and at the same time explained through the theatre. But at the same time the new theatre comes into being from a conflict about words themselves. In fact, the sovereignty of verbal meaning in the theatre brings out the imaginary. What is mimed, what is spoken, the tree, the rain or the moon only exist insofar as they are presented in a completely unreal manner. They lose any ability to react physically and realistically on the active senses of the public.

And we can see that with Artaud, who looked for new methods to reach the most profound depths of the spectator by using realistic conditioning factors (carefully worked out sounds and lighting) that from his first writings on the theatre, he assigned a secondary importance to language. In his 'theatre of cruelty' he says that he uses words, not so much for their meaning but for their actual sound. If I relate, as Corneille does, the murder of Pompey on the stage I diminish the effective force of the words because I dilute them in an imaginary story. Artaud says that when a word is spoken with force and emphasis in the right place under a certain light by a certain voice, produced by a free association of words that are not significant in themselves as for instance the word *murder*, the word *mother*, the word *blood* or a sexual word, it can directly affect the spectator and bring out directly, as in a psychoanalytical cure, all his unconscious verbal being. This attitude to language is very extreme. Between the theatre of Claudel, which delights in being what amounts to the organisation of 'intelligible dust' as he has put it, and the attitude of Artaud who subordinates the word to live action, there is a frank contradiction. The contemporary theatre offers different solutions, because of different preoccupations. The origin of this situation is undoubtedly the slow conviction which has overtaken us that 'the Freudian subconscious is organised like a language,' as Lacan puts it. What I mean is that the new playwrights start, more or less explicitly, from the same idea as Artaud, but the conception of language as the 'masked symbol of our destiny' becomes ever stronger for them. It must be said that for many contemporary authors Heidegger's phrase, whether they are familiar with it or not, appears to be true that 'man comports himself as if he was the creator and the master of language, whereas it is, to the contrary, language which is and which remains his master.' If we replace the word 'man' by 'character' we shall understand many of the experiments of the modern theatre. In the conversational theatre, even if the character does not say everything, even if the conversation is relegated to a sub-conversation, the author behaves as if his heroes and he himself were masters of language. They say and listen to what they wish consciously to express. But if, as many people think, language is master of man and it constitutes his personality and his destiny, if the laws of language, instead of being practical means of communication and of expressing ideas, were to appear, like physical laws, as pre-human and constituent necessities of man's existence, then the man of the theatre will no longer consider speech as a royal instrument which his heroes can make use of with abandon, but, on the contrary, he will want to show it as the master of man. That would be enough to change the significance and the value of theatrical prose. For Ionesco and those who follow him, language has a life of its own and is not at all the means that the hero chooses to express himself. On the contrary, it has the effect of showing him how it develops itself, without human help, independently of man, imposing its laws on him in spite of the effort of the speaker to make something clear, taking his meanings and pushing him further by the simple power of the word itself, into acts that he had no desire to commit and which are simply brought into being by the extent to which the word has power to design a course of action. In *The Lesson* the professor kills his pupil during the course of his lecture, an action which was certainly not part of his intentions at the beginning. And so, in the early plays of Ionesco, language is the hero and the principal character. It is king to exactly the extent that this type of theatre dethrones man. We are therefore talking about plays of language, but you can see how far removed they are from the plays of Claudel. They still contain characters, imaginary people, but they are intentionally weak, because they are nothing more than what is said about them and by them.

The theatre is losing its anthropomorphic quality and it is bringing into being what is called in a certain literature in France, a decentralization of the subject. We no longer have anything but a solitary and living object in front of us: language and conversation. Is this object real or imaginary? Are we on the side of Artaud's action or of Genet's verbal mirage? In reality Ionesco shows us everything as an intermediary solution. He tries to unveil language by making it speak by itself. But at the same time, he pushes it to absurdity at the same time as this absurdity proves itself logical. And so he denounces language as inhuman. For example, in the first speech of the *Bald Prima Donna*, a woman announces what she has been eating, talks of the English dishes that she has just had, because she is English and in England, says that she has eaten an English sauce and finishes by announcing 'we have drunk English water.' Now it is quite clear that all this is at the same time perfectly logical, because in her enumeration, all the dishes have been named in English, even to the English water! And also absurd, because although she is in England, this water is considered as a universal element. This manner by which the language continues is pushed by its logic to absurdity outside of the woman's will and contributes to making the language unreal, by showing us through exaggeration and by language which is itself unreal, that real language, that is to say the same language but not exaggerated, entirely contributes to the enslaving of man.

The theatre of immediacy, the classical theatre as it has become transformed into the bourgeois theatre, contains in itself contradictions of which it is not aware. For this reason, plays will differ in their content, but can all be referred to a certain form of theatre, comedy, tragedy, drama, melodrama, etc. The new theatre, the critical theatre has discovered the contradictions of its own nature, for instance, repetitive ceremonies, unusual events, spell-binding through the creation of illusions, through realistic conditioning and conditioning by a real action, by the glorification of the imaginary, by the sadism of reality, by man's mastery of language and by pan-verbalism, through the language which determines the destiny of man or by those simple means which are always betrayed by a conditioned subjectivism. These authors are all alike, although differing in their content, by the terms of the contradiction for which they have opted. Is this to say that the theatre is decomposing? No, but it is examining itself and deepening itself.

Far from the disaggregation of a new formula expressing disaggregation and a breaking apart into chaos, it represents the dialectical unity of the real contradictions that are present in art. If we look at them together, if we take the sum total of all the contemporary plays that they represent, we may have all of the theatre before us, not all of the theatre with its obscure contradictions, but certainly all of the theatre seen as a dialectical process which unites and progresses through its contradictions, and which is able at any particular moment to reconstitute its integral unity by the appearance of a work created out of these contradictions which supersedes them. For the rest, if we look at the entirety of plays for the new theatre, we can allege that they have certain common characteristics: these characteristics are negative ones which consist of a number of denials, but which are denials from which I believe we can draw some conclusions about their future unity. There are three essential refusals in the contemporary theatre, and they are the refusal of psychology, the refusal of plot and the refusal of all realism.

The Dialectic of Contradiction

All these authors have the same reasons for denying these three theatrical characteristics. In denying psychology they are denying the supremacy of the bourgeoisie, because the psychological theatre is essentially an ideological theatre that believes that man is not formed by his historical and social conditions, but that there is a psychological determinism and certain characteristics of human nature which are always the same. This is what is denied by all these authors, whether they are politically committed or not, simply because they believe that only the fundamental counts: whether this fundamental consists of language, or of being in the world, whether it consists of social existence in the profoundest sense of the word, just as long as it does not consist of the word games of psychology. The refusal of psychology is consequently followed by the desire, whether by means of the imagination or by brutal reality, to speak to and to understand our profoundest and real natures.

All these authors that I have named, far from being afraid of creating a scandal, want to provoke one as strongly as possible, because scandal must bring with it a certain disarray. I think that Beckett spoke for everyone when having presented his play *Waiting for Godot* and hearing the first night audience at the theatre applauding vigorously, said: 'Good God, there must be a mistake. It's not possible, they're applauding!' Because for all these authors in practice, whether they believe in the imaginary or in the real, they all believe that contact with the public can only be made after a scandal.

And for this same reason they refuse the convenience of having a plot. There are no longer any plots in the sense of little anecdotal stories, more or less well written and developed with a beginning, a middle and an end. These no longer exist because authors think that to entertain is to turn the audience's attention away from the essential point. Plots are there to give pleasure. They do not want to please. They want a subject, that is to say a whole situation which develops itself, and not formulae which can be used to construct an anecdote inside a story. They do not want the structural elements in a play, but want to build the subject as strongly as possible and the structure they build is based on the temporal nature the theatre itself. Their purpose is not to tell a little story, but to build a temporal object in which time, by its contradictions and by its own structure will put the theatre into relief in an especially concentrated way which then becomes the subject proper. And then they refuse realism simply because realism is at bottom a whole philosophy of which they want no part. First of all it is a philosophy which seems to them to be bourgeois, and then there is the whole idea that reality is realistic. Whereas in the true sense of the word reality is realistic only on the level of conversation. To put it another way, we adapt ourselves to the real when we talk about trivial things. On the level where they wish to be and which for all of them (whether their work is essentially comic, tragic or anguished) the level of subterranean motivations, or, if you prefer it, the level of human adventure, the essential conditions of human adventure are no longer realistic, because we can no longer understand them in a realistic way. We are unable to grasp the idea of death and we are unable to think about death, even if we are otherwise perfectly convinced, as I am, that death is a purely biological process, because even so, the sudden absence and the interrupted dialogue is something that we cannot subjectively realise. And so, when we wish to talk about life we cannot do so in a realistic way. If we wish to talk about birth, or our birth, an event that we have never lived through and which has nevertheless made us what we are, realism means nothing at all because we cannot realise the fact of our birth.

This triple denial of the world shows that the new theatre is not in fact absurd but that by its critical nature it returns to the great fundamental theme of all theatricality which is fundamentally man himself as an event, and man inside that event as a historical phenomenon.

(This text was given in Bonn as a lecture
on December 4th, 1966).

A Structure of Language

(An interview with Jean-Pierre Berckmans)

Brook's attempt (*US*) is interesting and will surely bear fruit, but it is incomplete. One might almost call it a piece of *poetic enthusiasm*. *US* is *shock-theatre* producing a *good* result because after all it does leave the audience in a state of frustration, it does expose the impotence of the Left, and this is a good thing; but there is clearly no ideology here, no objective conception defining a political line. If the Americans were to make peace in Vietnam I fail to see how this play could survive. It is too close to the event.

As far as I am concerned, then, it will be forgotten, whereas a play like Brecht's *Herr Puntila and his Man Matti* will live on ... at least until capitalism is a thing of the past.

What is there in positive terms that can be drawn here and now from Brook's theatrical formula?
Nothing, since the whole thing is negative. Except that, as Marx said, 'Shame is a revolutionary

sentiment,' and the shame which people of the Left may feel when they see this play and admit to themselves, 'Yes, we're utterly impotent,' may push them into objective action of a more useful kind.

Is there not a risk of pushing them into a pessimistic attitude?

I don't think so. The play is designed to irritate them, to provoke them. If it revealed their impotence in a *commiserative* way, then you would be right. But what it says to them is: 'You bastards!'

Provocation is something positive, then?

As soon as you provoke people, as soon as you make them feel uneasy, then you have done something good. And in fact, fundamentally, it is not the bourgeois who need to be made uneasy, it is the Left. There is in France a kind of clear conscience which is absolutely bourgeois. A play that provokes it, that says: 'If the Vietnam war is a filthy mess then you, the people of the Left, are another one,' is something salutary. It is just that with Brecht, who also did similar things, there was an ideological direction as well. Whereas with Brook it is all anger, it is all passion.

Do you see any theatre in the Artaud tradition which is able at the same time to represent a profound political argument?

No, because I find there is too much disorganization of meaning. There has to be meaning. The smallest step in the direction of Artaud's wanting to disorganize language and you've had it . . .

You believe there has to be a precise structure of language?

Yes. It does not matter which. Ionesco's is valid, just as Brecht's is. But you must not take words in their affective connotations without linking them together in a sentence. That was Artaud's mistake.

*In the case of the 'Living Theatre' you have the very way the group is constituted, its very way of life, representing a negation and rejection of traditional bourgeois society. The 'Living Theatre' thus 'argues' both in terms of its art (***The Brig, The Connection, Frankenstein***) and also in terms of the way the troupe lives. Does this represent an important trend in the modern theatre?*

To tell you the truth I regard this as a bit of a dilemma. What matters is the play. Whether or not the actors live on exemplary life, the impact on the audience occurs in and through the play. Now, you might say: 'Yes, but in order to be able to perform the play as they do, are they not obliged to live in a certain way?' That is precisely the problem, though. In point of fact there is a confusion here.

Remember that the actor is a person who temporarily discards his own reality; so it is not absolutely necessary that his life conform to the play he is acting in, in fact it makes absolutely no difference. Having said this, I am glad that they do live in the way they do because it shows that they are in fundamental agreement with their own ideas and so on. But as far as the actor's playing is concerned it is of no importance whatever. Taking this to the extreme, you might even, in a thoroughly revolutionary play, bring on for one reason or another a completely bourgeois actor who would yet play his role in such a way as genuinely to 'grip' the audience. It is the role that matters, you see. With us writers, for example, it is the other way round; I consider that we are under an obligation to live as we write. I could no longer allow myself to go on writing as I do if for example something happened in my private life to give me a feeling of guilt reaching a certain level. This is a case of strict necessity. With the actor it is different – and I say this with no disrespect for the acting profession.

A large part of all theatre in the Artaud tradition is based on the 'actor as creator'. In Brook's theatre in particular a great deal of the text is made up by the actors. This does require a powerful notion of group, does it not?

Yes, I am not against this trend. But I do wonder if there isn't some confusion here, whether Brook has not in fact taken a wrong turning, whether it isn't necessary to make a definite choice between the happening and representation in the Brechtian sense, whether this kind of patchwork really is something *genuine*, but nevertheless completely contained within certain moulds – or if it isn't simply a character rather like the actor in the old 'Commedia dell'Arte' who improvised on a skeleton plot.

Turning to the question of audience participation, in what way can such participation add to the message or content of a play?

First of all it varies very much. Some of the French happenings in particular leave the audience stupefied; others again put one in mind of the 'Folies-Bergère' (with a beautiful nude woman on the stage . . .); others are merely scandalous, making a purely visceral appeal. I am not sure whether, it many cases, any positive purpose is served. On the other hand you may have something which goes slightly beyond the happening — in a way this is the criticism of it — as when censorship steps in. For example an episode of a happening may be forbidden by the police. The actors comply but start to improvise against censorship, and in the end the whole thing turns into a demonstration. This is fine, but at the same time it represents a criticism of the happening because it needed an objective, external fact to make the transposition. In other words the public had to know that it was coming to watch a censored or censorable happening.

That is not unlike the Provos' theory — no successful, effective happening without police intervention.

Perfectly true. The happening must call into question the whole of society, and consequently also the forces of order, the bourgeoisie, etc. But it seems to me its value is extremely limited. Fundamentally it is just good old Surrealism once more. It seeks to bring to light all the forces that Surrealism classified as *surreality*, namely libido, pure imagination, infinite desire, etc. But we are a long way from any kind of political position here. For the happening to become political, it needs something other than itself.

There is one country where happenings always end on an emotional note which is profoundly political, and that is Japan. There is not a single

Japanese happening that does not revolve around the atom bomb, because of the memory of the past, and of the fear of the future. A Japanese director may very well stage a happening that has to do with sex, but it will always end with some kind of reminder of Hiroshima or Nagasaki.

What I am trying to get at is that basically the happening is still imaginary. A real event is a springboard for an imaginary reality. But not the happening: it believes that the real event refers back to real forces of the mind. In actual fact it is a symbol, a catalyst of an imaginary event. That is where the happening becomes theatre. But it must not be thought of as a real provocation. Fundamentally I agree with the Provos, but in a different sense: I would say that the happening disturbs the imagination of the bourgeois audience, and then a blow – a real blow – from a policeman's truncheon changes everything: you wake up again.

Let us take another kind of theatre, one which represents a compromise between action and representation, the theatre of Grotowski. This is a theatre offering a visceral solicitation to the individual, a staged 'act', but isn't the spectator relegated to the position of voyeur?

Exactly. I find that kind of theatre of no interest whatsoever. Of course the aesthetic interest, I grant you, may be considerable – it's beautiful, it's fascinating, but there is no element of *a posteriori* rational reflection on the part of the individual. Grotowski creates a visceral disturbance which simply goes on; there is no reason why it should trigger thought, and it is incapable of producing a suitable climate for any kind of intellectual or physical revolution . . .

If the fellow can go and beat up a policeman, all right, that's fine, but it won't produce any result. When all is said and done, I think theatre that is not associated with an ideology — indirectly, that is, because clearly a completely ideological theatre is somewhat risky (when Adamov says: 'No theatre without ideology,' he is going too far) — but theatre that is not associated with a particular ideology, theatre that seeks to shock in a diffuse manner, cannot make for revolution. Only a Trotskyist would believe it could — a Trotskyist of the old school. One would have to believe that all levels are mutually symbolic, that the political revolutionary level symbolizes the sexual revolutionary level, and *vice versa*. It is an idea I find attractive but erroneous.

Art, of its essence, is opposed to that which exists; its task is neither to glorify nor to explain; its value is one of terrorism; it is a weapon against traditional values and morality; it is aggressive, challenging, destructive; it leads established society to deny itself through the medium of the culture which it demands. This is the great lesson of de Sade and the true Surrealists.

Le Point, no. 8, February 1967

The Writer and his Language

(An interview with Pierre Verstraeten)

Does it make any sense to you to set yourself the problem of your relationship to the French language as a whole?

It certainly does make sense, yes, because I regard language as something we are *inside*. Language is a kind of vast reality, what I would call a *practico-inert* entity, and I am in constant touch with it — not in so far as I utter speech but precisely in so far as it is primarily, for me, something which encompasses me and from which I am able to take things. It is only subsequently that I discover its function, as communication.

So the first moment is one of exteriority?

Yes. I do not see language as being something which is inside me. I believe people say they have the impression, whatever they think afterwards, that there are words in their head. I don't. My impression is that they are outside me, like a sort of vast electronic system: you push certain buttons

and you can get certain results. And you mustn't
think this is the result of a thought process. I have
written something similar but I was writing with
reference to an experience which I would call both
objective and subjective. That's the starting-point,
then: I don't have the words inside me; they are
outside me.

Can you account for this feeling?

This is partly what I was saying in *Words*.[1] I
think it is because for a long time – when I was a
boy I believe this was so – I used to confuse words
with things. I mean that the word 'table' *was* the
table. When I began to write there was this classic
moment, but I didn't get any further. I always
thought that making the table mine meant finding
the word for table. So there was certainly a close
relationship between words and myself, but it was
a relationship of ownership. In my relationship to
language I was owner, I am owner. As a French-
man, the French language is my property, as it is
the property of every French-speaking person; I
have a feeling of possession as regards the French
language. Except that, as I am trying to explain, I
possess it, I own it, as something external to
myself. In fact I think it's the only thing I do own.
It is mine. This does not mean that it does not
belong to other people too – that is not the
problem – but I feel at home in my language; and
the difficulties I come up against there – enormous
difficulties – seem to me always to be difficulties
of expression, difficulties of administration if you

[1] Jean-Paul Sarte, *Words*, Hamish Hamilton, London, 1964.

like, and even if I do not succeed in overcoming them I know I ought to be able to. Its the attempt, if you like.

But this one might easily term a bourgeois relationship, might one not, since it is a property relationship?

Certainly in origin — which is why I say this — it is a bourgeois relationship.

And why is it not this relationship that springs most readily to the bourgeois mind, since, as you say, the majority of the bourgeoisie regards language more in terms of a kind of internal autonomy?

I suppose one's reasons would have to be somewhat analytical, in the sense that we have unclear options in childhood which correspond to transferences. What I mean is this: I was a middle-class child and never possessed anything; I had nothing, as a child, that was *mine*. To start with I lived with my grandparents, so I possessed only what was given me. Later on — my mother having re-married — I lived with a stepfather who supported us and who gave me what I had. And I had everything; I never wanted for anything, but nothing was ever *mine*. Consequently, as regards property in general, I remained completely free. I never 'caught' it, so to speak, because on the one hand I had everything and so never knew the bitterness of wanting, yet on the other hand I never had anything, I never possessed anything. There was always plenty, but of things which were not mine. So I think a transference took place. In the same way as I put God into literature at a certain point, so I think I invested words with ownership. I always thought that the word was a way of possessing the thing, and I believe this was originally a bourgeois idea of appropriation. Its first appearance was as a tool for taking possession, and only later did it become collective means of communication. Of course my age had something to do with it. Now it is a thing of the past, though this is partly just through my having grown older. But that was certainly the first thing. Language, then, is something belonging to me, half on the side of the thing signified and half on the side of the signifier, but external to them. The word 'table' is half in the table and half an instrumental extension of my resources.

So this would be a description of your current relationship to the French language, then, but at the same time it seems to correspond to what might have been your relationship to it in childhood. This would mean you have never outgrown that relationship . . .

Oh indeed yes. Obviously one outgrows it as soon as one starts to communicate. A part of every writer is still the child whose aim is not communication but this kind of creation-appropriation. One creates, through words, the 'table'; one utters the equivalent of the table and there one has it. The result is that you think that if you have written a few words, a few nice words that go well together — Flaubert believed this all his life — you

are appropriated within a certain space, a space
which is yours and which is at the same time your
relationship to God. You have uttered the equivalent of the table and the table is caught in the
trap; the equivalent, the trap, *is* the table. All of
this presupposes non-communication, because
when we say that writers only write for other
people this is true only in the long run; it is not
true originally. There is the definitely magical idea
of the word which makes one write for writing's
sake; you create words, or rather you create
combinations of words, just as a child might build
a sandcastle — for the beauty of the thing itself,
not in order to show it off. Or, if you do
subsequently put your words on show, as it were,
the readers are inessential, like the parents who are
brought along and told: 'Look what a lovely
sandcastle I've built!' The parents say: 'Oh, isn't
that a lovely sandcastle!' and the reader's role is
initially just that. Which is why you still find many
people who are shocked when you say: 'Yes, but
one writes in order to communicate.' They have
never got beyond a certain point in their verbal
childhood, you see. They reckon — as indeed
Flaubert wrote — that they can build a 'wordcastle'
which will stand up by itself. I think that, for the
writer, this is the first step. I do not think one
would be a writer if one had not at some time or
another dreamt of doing exactly that. But you
cannot really write, not even at the age of fifteen,
without that moment becoming eclipsed. There
comes a time when the question of contact begins
to occupy the foreground. The magical aspect of

language gradually disappears, and this represents also a disenchantment. As soon as you discover that the word is not designed to possess the table but to point it out to someone else, you have a certain collective relationship of translucence which puts you in touch with man, certainly, but which also relieves you of the Absolute. As in the case of any other kind of evolution, however, it is impossible to say at what point this occurs, or how much of the old belief survives in a residual form. For example, I am well aware of the fact that I write in two different manners, and curiously enough the clearest is the one which retains most of the residue: that is, my literary manner. The former belief comes out at the level of what I would call prose. If you like, it comes out in the fact that a prose-writer can never after all be purely and simply a man who points things out, who designates things; he is a man who does so *in a particular way*, in this 'captious' way, by means of certain kinds of words, a certain use of resonance, and so on. In short he is someone who, when all's said and done, does introduce into the sentence the object described. A writer of prose, when speaking of a table, will write certain words about that table but he will do so in such a way — in accordance with his purely subjective idea of the matter — that that combination of words constitutes a kind of reproduction or bodying-forth of the table, so that the table is as it were incarnate in the words. This table here, for example — if I were writing about it I should have to incorporate in the very structure of my sentence something corresponding to the way this wood is dented, split, heavy, and so on, none of which is at all necessary if it is purely a question of communication. When I am writing what is known as literary prose, then, that aspect is always present; otherwise there would be no point in writing in that language. On the other hand, the most difficult thing about philosophical communication is that it is purely a question of communication and nothing else. When I wrote *Being and Nothingness*[2] it was uniquely in order to communicate thoughts by means of symbols.

You have explained what is left over of the original belief. Can you also explain — technically, I mean — what there is that is new, as compared with writing which has never got beyond the stage of this 'former belief'?

What is new is a contradiction. You know that nowadays a distinction is made between 'people who write' (*écrivants*) and 'writers' (*écrivains*) — the latter being the *Tel Quel*[3] people, for example. The 'people who write' are those who explain things, who point things out, who write in order to designate objects. But there are other people who write in order that language as such shall become manifest — in its movement of

[2] Jean-Paul Sarte, *Being and Nothingness*, Methuen London, 1969.

[3] *Tel Quel*, a review founded in Paris by Philippe Sollers in the 1950's, has become not only the leading journal for certain forms of French literary and philosophical thought, but the centre of the movement for those who literary and philosophical outlook is based on linguistics and the theory of structuralism.

contradiction, of rhetoric, in its structures. These are the 'writers'. Personally I would say that life teaches one to go beyond both points of view. I do not think one can be a 'writer' without being a 'person who writes', and *vice versa*. Thus what was originally refusal to communicate or ignorance of the fact of communication at the time when I was making 'wordcastles' remains as a residue, as a kind of communication over and above the actual organs of communication. I mean that what interests me *now* is communicating with the reader. I am no longer interested in making an equivalent for the table through the relationships of words among themselves; what I want is for those words to produce in the reader's mind, through their mutual relationships, through the way in which they touch one another off, the table which is not there, not merely as a symbol but as a table which has been conjured up. I am trying to point out that the goal is always something that takes you back to the 'person who writes', at least as far as I am concerned. I want to say something, and I want to say it to other people, certain definite people, people who are either for or against ideas or courses of action in regard to which I occupy a particular position myself. To my mind the goal is in spite of everything this relationship with the other person. However, what distinguishes the 'writer' is that he is a person who believes that language is object of total communication, is means of total communication, and who believes this not in spite of the problems of language — the fact that one word has several meanings, or that syntax is often ambiguous — but because of them. What I mean is this: if you use words only in order to communicate, there is clearly a certain residuum, something not covered. That is to say, we have these symbols which designate an absent object and which are able to designate it as possessing such and such a meaning and furthermore as occupying such and such a concrete position in relation to other objects, but the symbols do not reproduce what one might call the 'flesh-and-blood' object, and the invariable conclusion — at least the conclusion drawn by a certain kind of linguistic pessimism — the invariable conclusion is that, by the very nature of language, there is always this residuum of incommunicability, this margin of incommunicability, varying in extent but ineluctably present. For example, I might describe my feelings in quite considerable detail, but beyond a certain point the reality of those feelings will no longer correspond to the manner in which I choose to articulate them. There are two reasons for this. Firstly, language as pure symbol can only designate the thing signified in strictly conceptual terms. Secondly, there are too many factors within ourselves by which language is conditioned; there is a relationship between signification and signifier and this is a retroactive, centripetal relationship by which words become changed. What we say always differs to a greater or lesser extent from what we want to say by virtue of the very fact that we use words to say it.

Do you draw a distinction between signification and the thing signified?

Yes, to me the thing signified is the object. Let me define language as I see it – which is not necessarily the way the linguists see it. This 'chair' is the object, hence it is the thing signified. Then there is signification. This is the logical entity constituted by words, the meaning of a sentence. When I say: 'This table is standing by the window,' I am alluding to a thing signified – the table – by means of significations which are my sentences constituted as a whole. Myself I regard as the signifier. The signification is the *noema* or correlative of all the vocal elements uttered.

Borrowing the terms employed by the Structuralists, one might say that signification is the product of the articulation of signifiers, themselves considered as non-articulated constituent elements; signification would be the unit of meaning which brings about the unification of the discontinuous data of your verbal material.

Exactly. The articulation of signifiers gives rise to signification which in turn aims at the thing signified, the whole process taking place against the background of an original, initial signifier. Well, as I was saying, taking signification as a whole you have on the one hand a blank shot at the thing signified, a conceptual shot which by virtue of that very fact has certain shortcomings, and on the other hand an over-loaded relationship to the signifier having a super-determinative effect on the sentence – I use words which themselves possess a history and stand in a particular relationship to language as a whole, a relationship which is neither pure nor simple, which is not strictly speaking that of a universal symbolism, words moreover which stand in a certain (also particular) historical relationship to myself. This is why it is usually maintained that the thing signified must remain outside; language is simply a collection of significations and those significations leave a certain number of things outside. For example, I may offer a whole series of significations concerning a particular feeling of mine or my emotional conformation with regard to a particular individual, but in actual fact, since I am already conditioned by my history in the words I use, the result is a kind of double usage: I use to designate myself words which on the one hand have been given an altered meaning by my own history and which on the other hand have different meanings with regard to the history of language as a whole. This is why there are people who say there is no such thing as equivalence, whereas in actual fact I think the writer is the person who says to himself that, thanks to all this, equivalence does occur. That's his job. That is what we call style.

Would it be right to say that the adherents of this pessimistic view represent a kind of literary positivism?
Yes, that would be literary positivism. Very broadly it is the bourgeois concept of the impossibility of communication through language, a concept you even find in Flaubert. Flaubert

wrote, but at the same time he believed that we are unable to communicate, which led him to create a body of significations which were themselves to constitute the object of literature.

The foundation of which would be in this case, as you said in your Mutualité lecture, God or Death, these being the two instances which deny on principle direct communication between men.[4]

Whereas in reality the 'writer who writes' — i.e. the genuine article, the man who possesses both dimensions (at least that is how I see it) — ought to make this contradiction the very stuff of his writing. Basically I think everything is expressible provided you find the right expression for it. But finding the right expression does not mean inventing grammar nor does it mean making up words — although this is permissible on occasion, of course it is, that is not the problem, that is always a secondary consideration. No what this means in reality is working with that aspect of the word which relates to its own history or to the signifier considered as history. This to some extent means working in the dark; one is none too sure of what one is doing. The literary task is as it were a twofold one: it involves aiming at signification while at the same time charging it with something which must give you things as present.

In that case I wonder how far you are able to distinguish this position from literary positivism.

[4] See *Que peut la Littérature?*, Collection 10/18, Paris, 1965, pp. 107-125.

The literary positivists appear to draw the immediate conclusion that the idea of being able to attain the thing signified and thus to communicate it is illusory – illusory, that is, in so far as the thing signified will in the last resort always be the product of a certain relativity – psychological, psycho-analytical, or even sociologico-historical – which predetermines or dictates the thing signified. With the result that, rather than run the risk of this relativity – i.e. write as if it did not exist *or write* with the means at their disposal, *overlooking the fact that fundamentally this represents a pragmatic approach to communication – they prefer to do without communication altogether in order to avoid the risk of self-delusion and above all in order to be able to assess how much may be preserved of literature as such, once this subjectivity or fundamental relativity connecting us to the thing signified has been exposed. In this sense, even if the work written from your point of view differed radically from the work written from the other point of view, your position would be basically analogous to that of literary positivism, the only difference being that the latter is more radical and less naive. In view of this, do you think it possible to draw a distinction of principle between the two positions?*

You see, I think that, as Merleau-Ponty says in connection with the Visible, the 'see-er', the person-who-sees, *is* visible and there is a relationship of being between seeing and visibility: it's the same thing. And I would say the same thing here: the signifier *is* signified, invariably, and consequently there is a very close relationship of being between the thing signified which signification misses, and the signifier who is at the same time signified by his signification.

Yes, there I quite agree with you, but in order to establish this you have to resort to ontology.
I know, but you must understand that the notion of subjectivity is one I seldom use except for purposes of defining limitation, i.e. to say: 'This is only subjective,' or: 'I lack sufficient factors to . . .' and so on. But as far as I am concerned there is no such thing as subjectivity; there are only internalization and exteriority. Every thing signified is a signifier and every signifier is a thing signified, that is to say that there is something about the object that signifies language, that appoints it to be language, that calls for it and that defines words, and at the same time there is something about signification, i.e. about language, that always refers back to the signifier and qualifies him historically, in his being. The result is that language appears to me — and here again you see that it is something outside me — language appears to me as that which designates me in so far as I attempt to designate the object.

And it is on this basis that you would draw a firm distinction between your position and that of literary positivism, since you consent to base your position on an initial understanding of man's relationship to being, i.e. on an ontology. Literary positivism on the other hand would reject such an ontology as all positivism rejects any thought which goes beyond what it considers to be the field of experience as immediately given, or at least as verifiable by results. However, also present in the literary movement represented by Tel Quel — *and in a broader sense in all those writers who subscribe to the ideas of Robbe-Grillet — over and above this theory of literary positivism (which incidentally has never been elaborated), a possibility of basing and even a certain tendency to base their conception of writing on the philosophy of Heidegger, or at least on the latest direction taken by Heidegger's philosophy, in which Being is generally understood as writing itself or as language. The way in which you have just described the* ~~18, man is to bear witness. That is not the problem as far as I am concerned. And, in this~~ *relationship of signification to the thing signified — in which moreover you referred to a work of Merleau-Ponty's written at a time when he was himself under the influence of Heidegger — prompts me to ask you how your position relates to Heidegger's conception of Being. And perhaps I might establish this distinction, or give it a chance of establishing itself, by saying that it seems to me that you posit total reciprocity between the signifier and that in the thing signified which provokes the signifier, whereas with Heidegger it is ultimately the thing signified, namely Being, which enjoys complete initiative in the summons to speech.*

Right. And for me, consequently, this represents an alienation. You feel this with Merleau-Ponty too to a certain extent: any retrograde relationship to Being, or any overture to Being which presupposes Being both behind and before that overture and as conditioning it, seems to me to represent an alienation. I mean that I reject Being as itself conditioning an overture to Being. I also reject — because it would be possible to erect a theory of structures on that basis — structuralism as being something behind me. I have nothing behind me. I believe that man is at the centre, or, if there are things behind him, that he internalizes them. There is nothing prior to man — except the animals, except man becoming himself, but there is nothing prior to him which is behind him and to which man is to bear witness. That is not the problem as far as I an concerned. And, in this sphere which I am talking about, I consider that, in fact, every investigation is depth of the object or of myself is conducted on the basis of a constant praxis whose tool and mediation is language. There is not primarily Being which must subsequently be testified to. There are men existing in a world in which the very fact of their existing prompts them to internalize depth, and hence to become deep themselves and at the same time to reflect that depth, which in a way only exists through them. Man does not create the world; he only notes that it is there. But from the mere fact that he establishes undefined connections between objects which are themselves of undefined quantity he internalizes his depth or externalizes himself as connection to create depth in the world. One might say that man is the depth of the world and

the world the depth of man, and all this occurs
normally through the medium of a certain type of
praxis, namely the use of these artefacts we call
words. Because one thing we tend to forget is that
a word is an artefact – a product of history
re-worked by myself. I pronounce it when I speak;
I trace its letters when I write; these are material
activities – material activities which themselves
mean something in terms of language. A word is
something you must love to write if you really
want to write like a 'writer', as they say. One feels
this with Flaubert, for example – this love of the
word as material object. I don't know whether
you've read Mannoni's article on Freud's rat man.[5]
It is interesting because it shows clearly that Freud
did not regard – it would have been idealism if he
had – the words which for example replace on
another in certain phantasms as symbols or
symbolic vehicles on the grouns of their possessing
a given form, but as real objects acting in a real
way upon man – in short, as material objects. I
mean that it is an actual, material resemblance
between syllables which acts materially upon man
to determine him. What you have initially is not
objects which vaguely resemble one another and
are charged with symbolism; what you have
initially is objects. This is extremely important.
Writing also implies loving a certain class of
object – objects which are designed to signify, and
hence to allude to something other than themselves, and which are at the same time themselves

[5] See *Les Temps modernes*, May 1965, no. 253; reprinted in
O. Mannoni, *Clefs pour l'Imaginaire*, Le Seuil, Paris, 1960.

objects. But this brings us back to the reader. I think reading — when it is a question of a literary work, for example a novel — always involves two things: grasping the signification and investing the material body of words, whether written — and hence visible — or spoken — and hence audible — with a somewhat obscure function which is that of directly presenting the object by giving it to you, *qua* symbol, as absent. To take an example, if you write: 'I was taking a walk; it was night,' the person who reads that finds in 'night' something which is in fact the presence of night, although he is reading two sentences which tell him: 'This isn't night.' As soon as you use the *imparfait* you are telling the person: 'It is not night at the moment, or if it is, then that is accidental; at any rate the night I am talking about is in the past.' And as the reader reads, that night is present to him through the word in so far as the word is a material reality charged with a combination of elements which are also work — general, historical work or personal work. The word has a kind of functional value in itself: the word 'night' I would call the essence of night. You have the significations, and you have the essence, the meaning. The fact that there are words which I would call 'charged with meaning' — they can be any words — is due solely to the position they occupy in the sentence. You might, while writing, find 'sternutation' a more amusing word to use at a certain point than 'sneezing'. Hence the position the word occupies in the sentence gives it a directly communicable quality which is what I would call its meaning. So that if you consider that basically you are doing this for the reader, in order to present directly and incarnate for him the thing signified, you are yourself obliged to accept, together with your words, the full, personal, historical change with which they are invested as far as you are oncerned, as well as the various altered meanings which they evince.

There is a kind of affinity, then, between the writer's love of words and the possibility of the reader's incarnating what you call their meaning. In a way it is the writer's love of words which, by objectifying itself into meaning for the reader's benefit, makes literary communication possible.

Exactly. It's the same thing. And when one reads over what one has written, of course — when I re-read a literary text I have written, I do so in order to find out what impression the reader is going to get from it. I become my own reader, not to re-read myself, but to re-read as it were the work of another. In other words the very task of literature, if one is working with style, consists in asking oneself: 'What is this combination of words, given the inherent weight of each word, going to add up to?' You try to stand back from it, to project yourself into the position of a reader who is starting from scratch, or rather who does not have your history but only his own.

So this meaning would be as it were the locus of the universal since it makes it possible to combine the writer's and the reader's experience?

Yes, it is the locus of the individual universal or the locus of the concrete universal. It is where really the deepest part of literary communication can take place. Obviously this is something we do not need in philosophy; we even have to avoid it. If I forget myself for a moment and use a literary turn of phrase in a philosophical work I always feel slightly that I am pulling a fast one on my reader; it is a breach of trust. I once wrote the sentence – remembered because of its literary aspect – *'L'homme est une passion inutile'* ('Man is a useless passion'). A case of breach of trust. I ought to have put that in strictly philosophical terms. In *A Critique of Dialectical Reason* I do not think I was guilty of breach of trust at all. There are two very different things at issue here. In the realm of literature this kind of thing does not constitute breach of trust because the reader is forewarned. He is forewarned the moment he buys the book; either it says 'a novel' on the cover, or he knows it is a novel, or he knows it is some kind of essay but one which is going to contain emotional as well as reasoned argument. He knows what he is after. If a particular word carries a charge which causes him to receive it in a way slightly different from the simple signification, he knows this is going to happen; this is what he is after and he has his guard up, so to speak. There is thus a threefold process of mediation here. Signification is a mediation between the signifier and the thing signified – and conversely between the thing signified and the signifier. The thing signified is a mediation between the signifier and signification,

signification and the signifier. And all this can only take place in the presence of the reader as mediation firstly between the thing signified and the signifier and secondly between signification and the signifier. There are three terms to the process. To put it another way, if you have lost the primary illusion of the object, the sandcastle I was talking about earlier, you can only derive pleasure from writing in so far as all your words yield up all their possible content of abstruseness, i.e. of meaning – because abstruseness in a word is always a deeper meaning – and this is something you can only bring about through the fact that your words are destined for another person. Or to put it another way, in order to write you have to enjoy writing. You cannot simply transcribe; otherwise you just give pure significations. What I am trying to pin down is what it is to try and write, to have a style. You have to enjoy doing it. And for you to enjoy it, your relationship with the reader must reveal to you, through the significations pure and simple which you are giving him, the meanings which they contain, and which have come down to you through your history, and must be such as to make it possible for you to play upon those meanings, that is to say to use them not in order to make them yours but in order that the reader may make them his. In the last resort the reader is a little bit – because you are intending everything for him – he is a little bit like an analyst.

A kind of developing agent, then! Couldn't one say on that basis that there is a primary Other who or which is in fact constituted, – *which is let us say the practico-inert or History as it has given rise to language, as it has given rise to it in you, for you, in a particular way, with a particular, distinctive flavour – and which has by that very fact become buried and as it were forgotten, once internalized, but which is also as it were re-activated by the intention of communicating or the desire to communicate with a contemporary Other in so far as such an intention or desire necessarily prompts in you and for you, as well as for him, the disclosure of the original Other?*

Precisely. In prose there is reciprocity; in the case of poetry I think the other person has a purely revelatory function – like a developing agent, as you say. I don't think the poetic intention implies communication to the same extent. It poetry the reader is essentially my witness to dredge those meanings out of me.

There is something deeply narcissistic about poetry, then?

There is something deeply narcissistic about poetry but it passes naturally through the other person. In prose, on the other hand, there is an element of narcissism but it is dominated by a need to communicate. It is more mediatized, that is to say it is transcended in the movement towards the other person – in whom, incidentally, you are also going to engender narcissism: your words will please him precisely because they throw him back on himself. This is what I call 'resonance'. Reading by resonance is one of the most widespread forms of reading and one of the most regrettable in so far as it is that and nothing else. I mean the reader who, coming across a particular sentence — say a sentence which lies quite outside the general intention of the work or which is perhaps intended as a jumping-off point to something else — the reader who suddenly feels himself resonate at that point is immediately turned in upon himself and away from the communication aimed at by the work as a whole. But this resonance is nevertheless essential, on condition that it be kept within certain limits, both by the reader and by the writer.

So the narcissism of poetry is simply a multiple narcissism, affecting not the author alone but also the reader. The reader's attitude to poetry is analogous to that of the poet as he writes. Wouldn't this mean that communication was as it were ruled out, since from both points of view the object of poetry would be a kind of self-satisfaction?
This is what I believe poetry is all about — or at least has been since Romanticism.

Does this imply a negative, depreciatory judgement on your part with regard to poetry?
Negative? No, merely descriptive.

But as soon as you introduce the idea of narcissism, the idea of non-communication, or the idea of an aesthetic Grand Mediator between consciousnesses to define poetry, there is a certain negative implication. How, in view of this, do you see the salvation of poetry?

I think it's extremely useful. The salvation of poetry lies in the fact that there is also prose; it lies in the fact of their being mutually complementary. In this sense prose is continually having to rediscover and re-establish itself as against poetry. Poetry is that which is transcended or dominated in prose, real prose I mean, i.e. that inner structure of words which throws us back upon ourselves, upon history, upon narcissism, and at the same time upon the practico-inert which takes on things one never intended to invest in it. In this respect prose is the going beyond poetry. But you could also say that poetry is the true recovery of what is for all of us a moment of solitude which can always be 'gone beyond' but to which we have to return, the moment when words mirror for us the monster of solitude that we are, but do so gently, with a certain complicity — that is what you are giving the reader. So it is a different kind of communication by narcissism: the reader is there only to resurrect the author in the deepest quality of his being, and this he can only do by himself becoming narcissistic and putting himself in the author's place.

So one would uphold the distinction you have always maintained between prose and poetry by saying that basically they both stand in a certain relationship to communication, i.e. to the other person, but that in the one case this relationship as it were the reverse of what it is in the other.

Neither activity is wholly exempt from communication, but whereas the one as it were swims against the current of communication – in order to restore to it its depth – prose on the other hand seeks to overcome the separation or, to put it more simply, to establish communication. It remains perhaps to understand the import of this twofold communication, so rich in comparison with the banal kind of communication which is effected by way of neutral or neutralized significations. You said earlier, in distinguishing literary communication from ordinary communication, that the former consisted in more than the simple communication of significations, i.e. that communication per se *was not enough to define literary prose. What, then, is left of 'communication' in the essence of the literary phenomenon?*

That kind of communication is not enough because what distinguishes prose is the fact that there is always an overflow, above and beyond mere signification. One might even say that everything overflows the banks of signification, and it is this 'everything' that forms the basis of communication, or at least of communication in depth. For example, if you ask me: 'What street am I in?' and I tell you what street you are in, a whole series of tacitly understood implications passes between us which if we cared to go into them in detail would bring in the whole world. In fact we remain on a strictly practical level where language confines itself to imparting information. But if language is to become true communication it must reflect at each moment our positions in the world, both respectively and comparatively. And this is something it only does in writing, in the writing of prose. Poetry is the breathing space, the moment in which one recollects oneself. As I said, this moment seems to me to be indispensable. I do not at all accept the idea that absolute communication would involve no moments of narcissistic solitude. There is this movement of expansion and contraction, dilation and retraction.

So there are two kinds of communication in depth, as it were: that which is effected by prose and which is so to speak prospective, and that effected by poetry, which is more retrospective. Does this in your view correspond to an anthropological structure? What I mean is, could one regard the movement of prospection − and hence prose − as being bound up with ·history, or becoming, or action, i.e. with commitment, whereas the movement of retrospection represents a more strictly reflective attitude in the sense that reflection or thought is more static in its very content, that is to say represents ultimately a kind of falling back on a structure which in turn cannot be 'gone beyond' − the former constituting the future anthropological structure, and the latter − that which is engendered or revealed by poetry − constituting the ontological structure from which one sets out? Does that express your view?

That seems to me definitely so and it effectively stresses the fact that you do after all have externalization of internalization and internalization of externalization. You might call it the moment of interiority. And in the case of poetry we can say that this moment becomes a stasis. But it is absolutely indispensable, rather like a kind of brief halt enabling one to go back to the phenomenon of interiority without ever losing sight of the phenomenon of externalization.

Does this moment fulfil an ethical function, as you see it?

Yes, in so far as for me the concrete universal must always imply a kind of self-awareness that is other than conceptual, a kind of self-awareness that is awareness of Wish, awareness of History. Take awareness of Wish, for example. As I see it, a wish necessarily utilizes the force of need, but whereas need is a simple requirement – the need to eat, and to eat no matter what so long as it is edible – wish is on the level of Epicurus' titillation, i.e. I need to eat this rather than that. As soon as I want to eat this rather than that, the thing I want to eat inevitably refers me back to the universe. Because basically if I detest oysters but love lobster, or *vice versa*, it is always for a reason which goes beyond oysters or lobsters themselves; there are certain relationships to life, relationships to whole hosts of things, which refer us back to ourselves at the same time as referring us back to the universe. Strictly speaking, then, this wish is not directly related to articulation, as Lacan says. It is not something capable of articulation. My language is incapable of designating my deep-seated wish, hence another non-positivist theory of non-communication – that one can never, except through vague approximations set in perspective, furnish by means of language an equivalent for the phenomenon of desire — whereas I maintain that one does furnish precisely such an equivalent in poetry and in that going beyond the kernel of meaning through signification which is prose. Particularly in poetry, though, one furnishes this equivalent through the use of words not in so far as these are uttered for their own sake but in so far as the level below articulation is at work in their very reality, i.e. in so far as the density of the word in fact refers us back precisely to what has insinuated itself into it without having produced it. There is no deliberate expression of wish. Articulation is not designed to express wish, but the wish insinuates itself into the articulation of it.

It's an attractive answer but I wonder whether in fact it is exempt from the pessimism of psycho-analytical theory. When you say that poetry succeeds in expressing wish, there I agree with you. But then wouldn't psycho-analytical theory also agree in saying that words can at a pinch express wish but that in no case can they master or control it; that is to say that poetry can reflect it, but it is reflection which, by virtue of poetry's character-istic complacency, remains wholly bound up with the dramaturgy of desire, whereas what you were suggesting just now was in the nature of a possible dialectical — and hence progressive — relationship between what is concealed in poetry and what is aimed at in prose, since prose is bound up with the future and is thus prospective, while poetry, being retrospective, is consequently elemental. In this sense one could, potentially and in the long run, envisage a possibility not so much of reconciliation as of a mutual — and hence modifying — placing in perspective of ontological solitude with equally ontological communication. In view of what you have just said, does this possibility still obtain?

But there's no difference! I don't think poetry is ever going to be a catharsis in itself; rather it reveals man to himself through meaning. There is meaning there. After all the poet is not the same as a man who is dreaming; the conscious intention of the poet's awareness lies very far above the material infrastructure of the dreamer's. Hence there is something there, something which is objectified in what I might call this almost silent relationship of the words one to another, and it is this something which strictly speaking makes the poem. But there has to be this moment before you can have the moment of prose.

It's a kind of twofold process, then, the one aspect being perhaps comparable to what Freud called the death instinct, i.e. this moment of desire or of meditation on desire which poetry succeeds in mastering with its own resources, that is to say without going beyond it but simply by testifying to it, and the second being like the life instinct, namely prose, though this can never completely emancipate itself from poetry.

A very good thing too, because it is precisely this that gives it its true meaning, in other words furnishes the concrete universal. You utilize your desires, you utilize the way the world is for you in order to go beyond these things to something else: that is the depth and density of the word. That is why I think there is nothing that cannot be said.

It's perhaps in this respect too that prose alone can be effective — and I mean 'effective' in the sense that it can bring about direct change in things and not merely change through lucidity. Poetry may show man what he is, may actually be his lucidity and awake in him areas of darkness of which he is not yet in control, whereas the power of prose lies in its superior effectiveness — superior to the mere presence of literary potential — which comes from giving man the possibility of a real coming to grips with the world. In this sense, as far as you are concerned, poetry can have nothing to do with the criteria of commitment.

We're talking about a particular kind of poetry here, namely modern poetry. There are of course other kinds — the poetry of the Spartan Tyrtaeus, for example, which was in effect a summons to war, consisting of heroic chants, etc., and there was a stream of rhetorical poetry running right through the nineteenth century, even within Romanticism. These were obviously something quite different. What we are talking about here is the poetry of today, which came slowly into being through the Romantic period and emerged fully with Nerval and Baudelaire. In this kind of poetry I think that the poetic moment is in fact always a pause. And to begin with it was very often a pause of self-pity, of complacency with self seen as wish, as desire. It is the moment when desire objectifies itself through words, but above and beyond their articulation. Take one of Baudelaire's prose-poems: he loves clouds, which signifies that he loves a certain kind of beyond, he expresses his dissatisfaction, etc., all of which is on an abstract level, but when he writes: '*Les nuages, les merveilleux nuages*' the position of '*merveilleux*' and the repetition of '*nuages*' give rise to something else, and that something else is something of him or of us.

You were saying earlier that philosophy represents as it were the complete, diametrical opposite of prose, and hence a fortiori of poetry. How do you see this kind of purity of conceptual communication, again in relation to the ordinary, commonplace prose of communication which we have succeeded in distinguishing from literary prose but which we ought also to distinguish from philosophical prose – in so far as this prose of ordinary communication can be regarded as being weak, over-simplified, and too pure as compared with the affective impact of literary language? Do you see the question? Because it may turn out to be necessary to do the opposite of what we were doing a moment ago, namely to show that this ordinary, everyday prose is itself too highly charged or pre-charged . . .

Well, what I would say is this: we all know, don't we, what this everyday prose is. It has nothing to do with philosophical prose at all, because curiously enough the most difficult language of all in a way is the language that is most concerned to communicate, namely philosophy. Take Hegel. If you read a sentence of Hegel's without knowing something of what Hegel was talking about you will not understand it. This is another problem. Because as I see it the point of philosophy — which is neither that of anthropology nor that of any kind of science of man, nor is it even that of history — is to come as close as possible, by means of conceptual approximation, to the level of the concrete universal as given us in prose. In fact literary prose seems to me to be the still immediate, not yet self-aware, totality, and philosophy ought to be powered by the ambition to attain that awareness while disposing only of concepts. Its aim is thus to forge concepts which grow steadily and cumulatively weightier until we finally have as it were a model of that which yields itself up directly to prose. One might cite a profound and true remark of Rousseau's in his *Confessions*, for example, as the ideal to be achieved conceptually when one is philosophizing. For example, he was with Mme de Warens; he often went off on his own for quite extended journeys but always came back to her. He wasn't happy. It was then that he became disaffected. He wrote: 'I was where I was, and went where I went, never further.' What he meant was: 'I was on a lead.' But you see the meaning that gives to his signification. You see how a sentence like that refers us to a whole host of things. It's a perfectly simple sentence. 'I was where I was . . .' There was no transcendence. And why was there no transcendence? Because of this immanent relationship with Mme de Warens. He could pretend there was transcendence, but wherever he went he was never anywhere but where he was. Or else there were just little transcendences, on loan. He was allowed to visit such and such a town; he went, and he came back. 'I was where I was, and went where I went, never further.' Turning the sentence round, what it meant was: 'When I am free, free to wander as I will, I always go further than I travel.' What does that mean — to 'go further than one travels'? That is when you have true transcendence. The sentence refers us to freedom, to immanence, to transcendence, to a whole host of things. And furthermore to the relationship that lay behind it, the love-relationship between two people.

Could one say that every philosophy is as it were the logics of a phenomenology of existence, with the paradox that usually this distinction, so central to philosophy, appears as the distinction between abstract and concrete? In Hegel's philosophy, phenomenology is the concrete of which logic is the abstract; logic, on this basis, can put into few words what phenomenology says in many. Here, though, it's the other way round, because it appears that the phenomenology of existence — i.e. the sentence as it stands in Rousseau's Confessions *and the whole experience it covers — has to be minted in philosophical language of much greater length and complexity than the simplicity of the actual sentence.*

Yes, certainly it does, because you have to

rediscover that sentence and give it a foundation.
That's the problem.

The paradox I wish to point out, though, is this:
why is it that the foundation may turn out to be
more prolix than the thing itself?
Precisely because philosophy has to reject meaning.
It has to reject it because it must search for it.
Desire is expressible but, as we have seen,
indirectly, as meaning through words. That is the
density of words. But in the same way one can say
that experience, in the sense in which it is written
in prose, is incapable of articulation for philosophy
from the word go precisely because philosophy is a
matter of borrowing and inventing concepts which
progressively, through a kind of dialectic, bring us
to a broader awareness of ourselves on the
experiential level. Ultimately philosophy is always
designed to cancel itself out. I don't mean cancel
itself out in the sense in which Marx said there
would come a day when there would be no
philosophy. But the necessity of philosophy being
the acquisition of awareness, the moment one
could say that a man was totally aware of all he
was saying and all he felt when he said: 'I was
where I was, and went where I went, never
further,' – as Rousseau was not – in other words if
at that moment he could preserve the concrete
density of experience as expressed in literary prose
while at the same time being aware of it
conceptually, that would mean that he had not
only defined his relationship to the other person
and his relationship to himself but gone beyond

that to something else. What this amounts to is that philosophy must continually be destroying itself and being reborn. Philosophy is thought in so far as thought is invariably already the dead moment of praxis since, by the time it occurs, praxis is already framed. To put it another way, philosophy comes after, while none the less constantly looking forward. It must not allow itself to dispose of anything other than concepts, i.e. words. Yet even so what counts in philosophy's favour is the fact that those words are not completely defined. The ambiguity of the philosophical word does after all offer something which can be used to go further. It can be used in order to mystify, as Heidegger often does, but it can also be used for the purposes of prospecting, as he uses it also.

This would be how one would differentiate philosophical from scientific language, would it?
Exactly. Scientific language is pure application, action, and knowledge in the technical sense of the term. It makes no reference to man. Incidentally, speaking generally, anthropology is in my opinion a science which is destructive of man in so far as it deals with him exclusively or at any rate increasingly on the assumption that he is a scientific object and hence on the assumption that he is not also the creator of the sciences. Philosophy is concerned with the creator of the sciences and it cannot deal with him in scientific words; it can only deal with him in ambiguous words. Husserl's conception of philosophy as '*strenge Wissenschaft*',

a 'rigorous science', seems to me the idea of a madman of genius, but a mad idea none the less. At any rate you couldn't have anything more ambiguous than everything Husserl wrote. If you try to take Husserl's theory of *hule* as being a scientific theory when in fact it is capable of I don't know how many different interpretations, or if you look at his notion of passive synthesis, which is an extremely profound one but which occurred to him as a stop-gap — that's how one thinks in philosophy: it's not necessarily the dominant idea which is the best one — if you weight all this up, then, you see that the idea of philosophy being a 'rigorous science' makes no sense. Yet on the other hand, precisely because philosophy always contains concealed literary prose, ambiguity of terms, any terms, the concept is interesting because it retains a depth which does allow it, through those ambiguities, to get a tighter grip on that sentence of literary prose which already contains — but in a condensed form, not as yet aware of itself — the meaning which it will be philosophy's task to render.

While we're on the subject, what is your opinion of the criticisms that have been levelled at your adaptation of German philosophical language in Being and Nothingness, *criticisms which virtually pose a problem of translation? I imagine you consider the reproach unfounded, but how would you justify this kind of transcription of German philosophical language into French philosophical language?*

Once again, I consider that everything must be capable of being said. In this sense I am opposed to the kind of literary positivism which we were discussing earlier and which in the long run would amount to saying that it is impossible to translate Heidegger into French. Taking their stand on structuralism, the positivists would maintain that languages have no equivalence, that every language conditions itself as a whole, etc. This would lead on to the idea that the inventive part of Heidegger's language is consistent (which is true) with the German language. When he uses the word *Dasein* or the word *Bewusstsein*, or when Husserl uses the word *Bewusstsein*, you have there two ways of saying something to which nothing in the French language corresponds. And you would be forced to conclude that it was therefore impossible to translate, or else that this could only be done by means of cumbersome circumlocutions, which amounts to the same thing. Consequently, if we want to be able to say everything, if we consider that the thought of a German philosopher such as Heidegger ought to be accessible to us, even though we may not know his language, and if at the same time we believe to some extent that languages are entities which condition themselves internally and that one is not necessarily going to find the same things from one language to another, we have to concede that we must be allowed to do a certain amount of violence to language, our language, and make it say things which are perhaps 'not French'. For example, if you translate '*Dasein*' — it's not the Heideggerian sense, but it is a different sense – by '*être-là*', with the hyphen, the *être-là* (being-there) of a thing, it's not French. If you use the words '*existential*' and '*existentiel*' to distinguish two nuances which are constantly cropping up in German philosophy, it's not French. You can invent words in French, but it must be done in conformity with what we call the spirit of the language, that is to say in line with literary tradition as a whole, or rather in the context of a linguistic system's internal, dynamic relationships. So that when the poet invents words – as Léon-Paul Fargue did, for example, or as Michaux did – those inventions pass into the language. That is why the inventions of the philosopher who is seeking to import and acclimatize philosophical notions conceived by a German who has strictly speaking taken his language and given it a push in the direction in which it was going anyway – that is why the words which he invents will not necessarily align with the direction of the French language.

And do you consider you have escaped this charge?
No, no, on the contrary, I think I asked for it, I think you have to, because here you're introducing the concept. The concept is not susceptible of being broken away or separated from the word that expresses it. The idea of thought without words makes no sense to me at all. You have, then, a concept forged in German by means of an alteration in the German language, i.e. it became necessary to invent that concept. The concept manifested itself at a certain point as a lacuna in

Heidegger's thought and in order to pin it down Heidegger changed the meaning of a word. The nuance cannot be a purely German nuance since the thing at issue is after all a concrete universal. I am unable to give it an equivalent French word, then, or an invented word that shall lie truly in the traditional spirit of the language, and yet I need to. So what I do is this: I introduce a German concept by means of an un-French deformation of words within the context of a thought, in so far as thought is in fact more universal than language. There is one absolutely striking thing here: I do not know German very well in the original and only understand it with difficulty in translation, even when the translation is an excellent one. But that doesn't matter in the least, because afterwards the difficulty just disappears.

Couldn't one also say that, in so far as these concepts possess a creative or originative function, it might even be an advantage to the French reader to have as it were actually to come to grips with the word, precisely because it is a question of his making an effort to understand something new?
I would add, however, that, as techniques improve, so teachers will improve and increase the potential of expression, and the result of this collective effort will be that in ten years' time it will be possible to express the same thought very much more clearly and in very much simpler terms. Here we are talking about the moment of initiation: you are compelled to fill a gap in thought by doing violence to a particular language. Certainly, in this

sense, not all the words I drew from the German and used in this way are entirely satisfactory. But I'm not alone in this. Look at any translation of Heidegger, look at any translation of Schiller or even of Hegel and you will find expressions which the translators have obtained by forcing the language. It gives one a nasty feeling, this sort of thing, a sense of ugliness, which I believe one ought to disregard, but it also gives one a feeling of having been enriched, precisely because the concrete universal of philosophy is broader than the narrow domain of a particular language.

While we're on this point, your Critique of Dialectical Reason *could be said to owe very much less to German philosophical language. Yet here too criticisms have been levelled against you, though not of the same order since in this case no one could point directly to a particular influence. The writing in* A Critique of Dialectical Reason *has been described as clumsy, heavy-handed, interminable, involved, etc. Could one in this context talk in terms of this kind of writing being functionally necessary in view of the subject dealt with? I am thinking of Lévi-Strauss' remarks when he said that basically all writing – possibly he said all thought, but it comes to the same since, as you were saying just now, there is no thought without words, without writing – that all thought is analytical, and asked what right Sartre had to write a book dealing with dialectics in an analytical discourse when with his dialectics he claimed to be going beyond or to be furnishing the basis for analytics. I am thinking too of what — on a different level this time — Saint-John Perse said, to the effect that the French language is fundamentally synthetic, as compared to English, which is analytic. In other words, do you consider, on the one hand, that the writing in* A Critique of Dialectical Reason *is in terms of material structure peculiarly specific to its object, i.e. to dialectics, and on the other hand that, at the philosophical level as well as at the literary level in general, the French language has greater dialectical or synthetical potential that other languages — English, as Saint-John Perse believes, in particular?*

Firstly, let me be frank — I could certainly have written *A Critique of Dialectical Reason* better. These are purely anecdotal questions. By that I mean that if I had read it through again, cutting and tightening, it might not have given such a dense impression. From this point of view, then, we ought not to leave anecdote and the individual entirely out of account. However, this piece of self-criticism aside, the book would still have been much the same as it is because the basic reason why each sentence is so long, and bristles with parentheses, inverted commas, 'in so far as', etc., is that each sentence represents one whole dialectical movement. Lévi-Strauss does not know what dialectical thought is. Not only that — he is incapable of knowing. A man who writes the dialectics of that dichotomy is obviously totally incapable of understanding a dialectical thought. A dialectical thought is first of all, on one and the same movement, the examination of a reality in so far as it forms part of a whole, in so far as it denies that whole, in so far as that whole comprises it, conditions it, and denies it; in so far, consequently, as it is both positive and negative with regard to the whole, in so far as its movement must be both destructive and conservative with regard to the whole; in so far as it has a relationship to each of the parts of the whole, each of which is both a negation of the whole and includes the whole in itself; in so far as all these parts, or the sum of these parts, at a given moment denies — in so far as each contains the whole — the part we are considering, in so far as this part denies them, in so far as the sum of the parts, in re-becoming collectivity, becomes the collectivity of those parts joined together, i.e. the whole less this one, in conflict with this one, and lastly in so far as all of this, considered each time as positive and as negative, gives rise to a movement towards a restructuring of the whole. How can anyone expect all that, in connection with whatever moment of history one is expounding, or whatever moment of that moment — how can anyone expect all that to be expressed otherwise than in sentences of fifteen or twenty lines? And how can Lévi-Strauss say: 'Thought is analytical, therefore why adopt a dialectical form?' when dialectics is not the opposite of analytics but the verification of analytics in the name of a totality?

I think that what he would say would be not: 'Why adopt a dialectical form?' but: 'It is not possible to adopt a dialectical form.'

I'd like to see him prove it. You see, the very fact of him saying it shows that he does not understand what I am talking about, and in point of fact you never – in kinship ties, for example – you never have dialectics. That is to say you never have a fact studied in so far as it constitutes on the one hand positive negation of the whole or dependence upon the whole, and the reverse. You never get the process of dialectical inversion, which is absolutely essential to dialectics. In other words, directly you start considering a particular part as positive and consequently as a kind of totalization of the whole in itself, since the part contains the whole, you have to invert and show the whole as negation of the part in so far as all determination is negation. You must always have both things. But this kind of thought is non-existent in Lévi-Strauss' work. Dialectical thought is quite simply a way of using analytical thought; it is a dialectical use of it. This is what I tried to explain in *A Critique of Dialectical Reason*. Dialectical thought is not opposed to analytical thought. Analytical thought is thought that renders itself inert so as to be competent to deal with the inert, whereas dialectical thought is the synthetic utilization of the collectivity of inert thoughts which themselves become parts of a whole which shatter their determination and negation in order to re-belong to the whole, etc. So how can you help having sentences which are extremely long, seeing that dialectics is precisely the utilization of analytical sentences?

Yes, but this utilization, in so far as it is itself both constitution and destruction of the whole, operates at the level of the thing signified: when you say that you explained this in A Critique of Dialectical Reason, *you explained it by saying it, by signifying it, But what is important here, I think, is to bear in mind that you also demonstrated it in the very fact of your writing, through the material dimension of your writing. There is a kind of analogy here, then, between as it were the formal aspect of writing and its content.*

As I said, the requisite self-criticism aside, the book could not have been written otherwise.

So dialectical writing today inevitably does violence to the language as it exists?

At that level, yes. And it doesn't matter in the least. It would anyway.

No, it doesn't matter, but it's significant because after all it does define language as a stratum of inertia.

It is the practico-inert, that is to say a material field entirely constituted by a certain ideology or a certain ideological tradition, by a certain type of history which has brought things to pass in one way or another, but in any event I don't think there is any one language that lends itself better — or worse, for that matter — than any other to dialectical treatment.

So you would reject the idea that the French language is better endowed for the purposes of

synthesis, as compared to any other?
Yes. At the present stage of linguistic development that seems to me to be stupid.

In your opinion and in your experience, what kinds of trap does the tradition of the French language lay as far as your own projects are concerned? You have shown, for example – this is what we began with – that we are immersed in language, but what are the consequences of this immersion going to be with regard to the French language as such? You have pointed out that for Sade, for example, the word 'nature' was a trap which, in spite of all his efforts, he failed to avoid, and that one can see how he went beyond that trap, even while confirming its existence.[6] Have you experienced any such trap yourself, and have you succeeded in avoiding it? It could only be a question of dead traps, by which I mean sprung traps.

Considering the fact that in Sade's day the word 'nature' was the thing trapped since ultimately it was a particular way – and an extremely complex way – of expressing certain aspirations and conditions of contemporary society as a whole, one would have to look for modern equivalents . . .

Well, let me give you an example which has struck me in your writing – the use of concepts which, as a rule, and a priori, are precluded from your work but which crop up again in certain polemical pieces

[6] See 'Questions de méthode', in *Critique de la Raison dialectique*, Gallimard, Paris, 1960.

or in pieces which lie closer to the spoken word,
for example the word 'intelligence', or the word
'will', or the word 'energy', or the word 'courage'.
These are terms you have no hesitation in
employing.

Yes, but it all depends on where and how. I don't
believe I have ever used the word 'will' without
giving it inverted commas — that is to say theoretical inverted commas, invisible ones. We're not
talking about the novels here, we're talking about
essays, aren't we, because if Mathieu says: 'I have
no will,' we leave it up to him. No, I think I have
only ever used these words in political texts.

Polemical ones, too. For example you have no
hesitation in saying: 'The fellow is intelligent but
he's wrong.'

Yes, that I would say. I'd even say he is stupid
sometimes, if he is unintelligent.

Exactly. And yet you have shown elsewhere that
intelligence is always in the final analysis the
product of a particular situation, a certain relation-
ship to the world, etc. But here you seem to be
treating it as an intrinsic value, in the most classic
tradition of the psychology of the faculties.

I would even say that stupidity is a consequence of
oppression, to my mind, and that there is no other
stupidity but oppression. Jouhandeau once wrote:
'Fools do not always wear the air of oppression
that suits them,' which strikes me as an excellent
sentence. Yes, but I'll be frank with you: that's a
part of style, or *mauvaise foi*. It doesn't amount to

anything, as far as I'm concerned, except a weapon to use against the adversary.

Then it wouldn't amount to one of the difficulties or one of the problems which the French language presents to you?
Intelligence has never preoccupied me as a philosophical problem. It is indefinable. It does not mean anything; intelligence tests do not mean anything. A philosopher friend of ours recently wrote an extraordinary sentence in a letter to Simone de Beauvoir. She wrote: 'Anglo-Saxon psychologists maintain that there is an 80% incidence of heredity of intelligence.' That seems to me truly monstrous, don't you agree? One thing I should point out is that after all I write in so many different languages that things pass from one to another; I write the language of prose, I write the language of philosophy, I write the language of theatre, and so on.

It has become traditional to regard the French and English languages as being in some way different. Is it not of some consequence, for example, that French is a language with a great cultural tradition and that the majority of the writers whom we know have been to university – as is not the case in America, for example, which to some extent accounts for the special character of American literature? Do you regard this distinction as a pertinent one and what importance do you attach to it, because basically I think this is what Saint-John Perse was alluding to?

Firstly I would regard French not as being much more synthetical but as being much more analytical. But I would go further and say that, the problem being fundamentally the same, namely to furnish meanings above and beyond the process of signification, it is on this level that the problem ought to be considered. When I take up an Anglo-Saxon word which possesses a synthetic quality, i.e. one which contains within itself a whole host of things, or when I think of how simplified Anglo-Saxon syntax is, I sometimes think I would rather express myself in English than in French — precisely because one experiences a certain difficulty in conveying the synthetical in French, French being basically an analytical language. And also because one has to look much harder, one has to forage around much more in what I call meaning, in what I referred to a while back as the relationship between signification and the signifier, one has to explore all these areas of shadow, and one must exploit silence too; in short, because all this sets me problems as a craftsman — not as an artist; that does not make much sense to my mind — we are dealing with related problems. You will say that perhaps it requires more analytical thought to write in English, whereas we have to load our words more to convey a synthesis which has a tendency to leak all over the place. But the tasks are comparable. There are slight differences but they do not prevent writers in either language from saying what they have to say, what they want to and are able to say, even at the expense of what I described as distortion of the tradition of the language. One must be able to write what one wants to — and don't take my use of the word 'want' as a trap . . . I mean one must be able to express everything by this means, and this is what seems to me to be essential.

To sum up, then, you would regard language much more as a means than as an end?
I think so, yes, but at the same time I recognise that things only become interesting for the writer in that moment when the means is itself regarded as an end. The in-between moment, when you search as one searches a palette for the right colours, when you are in the act of hunting up your words, is still the one that gives the greatest pleasure. But obviously it must be only a means: it is the activity of mediation.

Revue d'esthétique, July-December 1965
Reprinted in *Situations IX*, Paris, 1972

Signature is a new series of shorter works, distinguished by the highly personal and imaginative approach of the author to his subject. It comprises works of poetry and prose, fiction and non-fiction, and includes English, American and translated texts.

		cloth	paper
Signature 1 DARKER ENDS by Robert Nye	*poems*	£1.05	50p
Signature 2 OLT by Kenneth Gangemi	*novel*	£1.05	50p
Signature 3 THE CARNAL MYTH by Edward Dahlberg	*essay*	£1.50	75p
Signature 4 THE THEATRE AND ITS DOUBLE by Antonin Artaud	*essays*	£1.05	
Signature 5 SHARDS by Nicholas Rawson	*prose poem*	£2.25	
Signature 6 ENEMIES by Reinhard Lettau	*sketches*	£1.75	
Signature 7 REFLECTIONS by Mark Insingel	*novel*	£1.50	60p